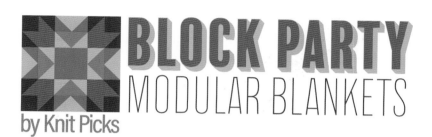

BLOCK PARTY
MODULAR BLANKETS
by Knit Picks

Photography by John Cranford
Graphic Design by Lee Meredith

Printed in the United States of America
First Printing, 2020

ISBN 978-1-62767-302-0

Versa Press, Inc.

800-447-7829
www.versapress.com

CONTENTS

BUFFALO

by Rebecca Minner

FINISHED MEASUREMENTS

52″ × 68″

YARN

Mighty Stitch™ (worsted weight,
80% Acrylic, 20% Superwash Wool;
208 yards/100g):
C1 Love Letter 28066, 11 skeins;
C2 Black 26852, 6 skeins;
C3 White 26807, 5 skeins

NEEDLES

US 8 (5mm) straight or circular needles,
or size to obtain gauge

NOTIONS

Yarn Needle
Stitch Markers
Locking Stitch Markers, optional

GAUGE

19 sts and 38 rows = 4″ in Garter Stitch,
unblocked (gauge is not crucial, but it
will affect finished size and yardage
requirements)

For pattern support, contact ampersanddesignsco@gmail.com

Buffalo

Notes:

Inspired by traditional gingham and buffalo check designs in woven fabrics, this modular blanket is a fun, oversized reminder of picnics and cozy flannel. It's truly a throw for all seasons!

Buffalo is a straightforward mitered square throw in which the buffalo check design element is made simply by changing the colors of the blocks as they are worked. The throw is started at one corner and worked to the opposite corner. It can be worked to any size.

Square blocks are viewed as diamonds; each will be 4″×4″. Instructions to pick up stitches from top left edge and top right edge are with right side up, and bind off of previous squares at the tops of diamonds.

The provided diagram has the first 24 blocks numbered in the order in which they were worked for the sample, to establish the construction, but they can be worked in many ways. The exact order the blocks are worked is not critical for the project.

Block Pattern
Row 1 (WS): K19, PM, K19.
Row 2 (RS): K to 2 sts before M, K2tog, SM, SSK, K to end. 2 sts dec.
Row 3: K across.
Rep Rows 2–3 16 more times. 4 sts.
Row 36 (RS): K2tog, remove M, SSK.
BO remaining 2 sts.

DIRECTIONS

Setup Block
Using C2, CO 38 sts.
Work Block Pattern.

Blanket
Rep Right Edge Block, Left Edge Block, and Center Block, following diagram to achieve buffalo design.

Right Edge Block
With RS of work up, CO 19 sts, PU and K 19 sts from top right edge of completed block.
Work Block Pattern.

Left Edge Block
With RS of work up, PU and K 19 sts from top left edge of completed block, CO 19 sts.
Work Block Pattern.

Center Block
With RS of work up, PU and K 19 sts from top left edge of completed block, PU and K 19 sts from top right edge of adjacent completed block.
Work Block Pattern.

Finishing
Weave in ends, wash, and block to measurements.

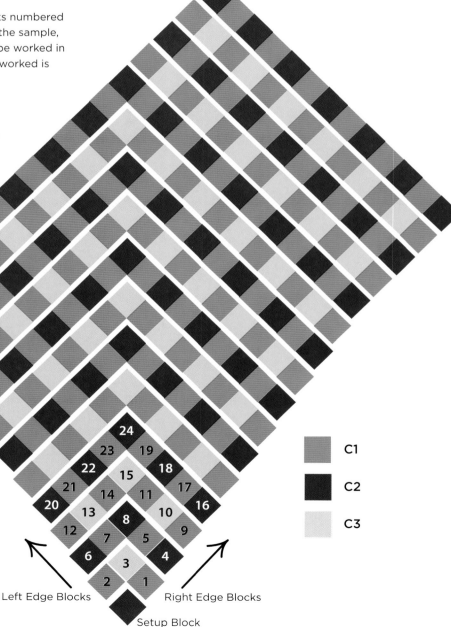

C1
C2
C3

Left Edge Blocks · Right Edge Blocks

Setup Block

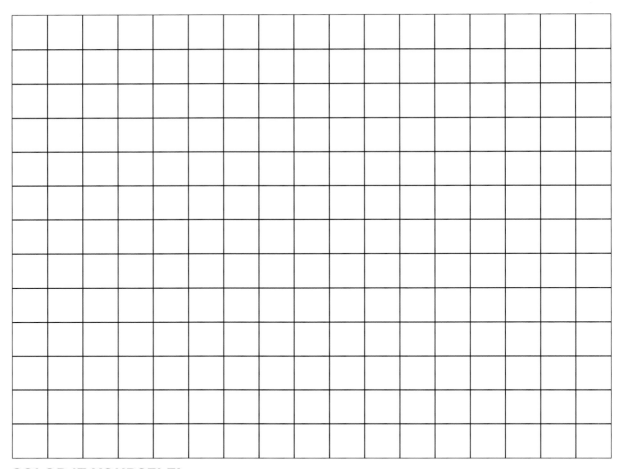

COLOR IT YOURSELF!

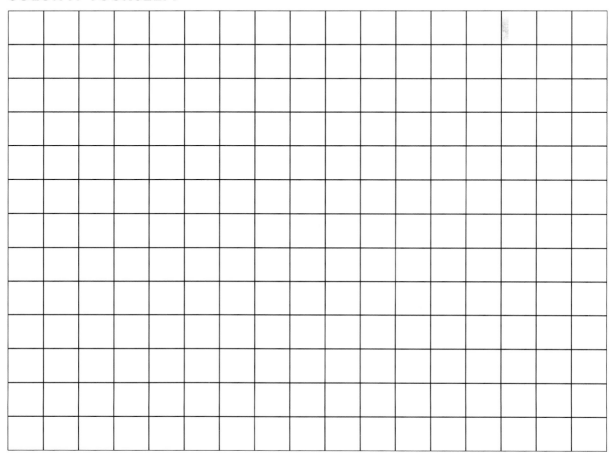

CLOUDY DAY

by Emily Kintigh

FINISHED MEASUREMENTS

Throw 45.5" × 59"
Pillow 16" square

YARN

Swish™ (worsted weight, 100% Fine
Superwash Merino Wool; 110 yards/50g):
Throw
C1 Cobblestone Heather 24661, 13 skeins;
C2 Dove Heather 25631, 11 skeins;
C3 White 24662, 3 skeins;
C4 Black 23876, 5 skeins
Pillow
C1 Cobblestone Heather 24661, 2 skeins;
C2 Dove Heather 25631, 2 skeins;
C3 White 24662, 1 skein;
C4 Black 23876, 2 skeins

NEEDLES

US 7 (4.5mm) straight or circular
needles, or size to obtain gauge

NOTIONS

Yarn Needle
G-6 (4mm) Crochet Hook
For Pillow: 16" Foam Pillow Insert

GAUGE

21 sts and 42 rows = 4" in Garter Stitch,
blocked

For pattern support, contact auntieemsstudio@gmail.com

Cloudy Day

Notes:

This lovely blanket will warm up the cloudiest days. The beautiful use of black, grays, and white are inspired by the clouds and a stormy sky.

Garter Stitch squares are shaped using simple increases and decreases. Four smaller squares make up one bigger square: two small squares are knit, then two more are joined to the first two as they are worked. A Garter Stitch border is added at the end and joined as it is worked.

Directions are also included for making a matching pillow.

Crochet Cast On

Make a slip knot with working yarn and place on crochet hook. *With knitting needle on left and crochet hook on right, bring yarn around back of needle. Reach hook over needle to grab yarn and pull through loop on hook. 1 st is now CO. Rep from * until there is 1 st fewer than desired CO number. Sl st from crochet hook onto needle.

THROW DIRECTIONS

Square A (make 24 the same)
Increase Section
With C1, CO 2 sts.
Row 1 (RS): K across.
Row 2 (WS): KFB twice. 4 sts.
Row 3: K across.
Row 4: K1, M1R, K to last st, M1L, K1. 2 sts inc.
Rep Rows 3–4 seven more times. 20 sts.
Break C1, join C2.
Work Rows 3–4 15 times. 50 sts.

Decrease Section
Break C2, join C1.
Rows 1–2: K across.
Row 3 (RS): K2tog, K to last 2 sts, SSK. 2 sts dec.
Row 4 (WS): K across.
Rep Rows 3–4 13 more times. 22 sts.
Break C1, join C3.
Work Rows 3–4 nine times. 4 sts.
Next Row: K2tog, SSK. 2 sts.
Break yarn and pull through remaining sts.

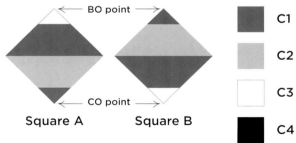

Square A   Square B

	C1
	C2
	C3
	C4

Square B (make 24 the same)
Each Square B joins tog two Square As while being worked. Once the first Square B is complete and the two Square As are connected, rep on the other side so that the four smaller squares make one bigger square.

Increase Section
With C3, CO 2 sts.
Row 1 (RS): K across.
Row 2 (WS): KFB twice. 4 sts.

Row 3: Lay out two Square As with RSs up and CO points touching; with LH needle, PU first Garter ridge st from CO point of LH edge of square on the right, then K2tog (first st tog with PU st); K to last st; Sl1 K-wise, with RH needle, PU first Garter ridge st from CO point of RH edge of square on the left, then complete SSK to work slipped st and PU st tog TBL.

Row 4: K1, M1R, K to last st, M1L, K1. 2 sts inc.

Row 5: With LH needle, PU st at end of next Garter ridge on LH edge of square on the right, then K2tog (first st with PU st); K to last st; Sl1 K-wise, with RH needle, PU st at end of next Garter ridge on RH edge of square on the left, then complete SSK to work slipped st and PU st tog TBL.

Rep Rows 4–5 six more times. 18 sts.

Rep Row 4 once more. 20 sts.

Break C3, join C1.

Work Row 5.

Work Rows 4–5 14 times. 48 sts.

Rep Row 4 once more. 50 sts.

Break C1, join C2.

Work Row 5.

Decrease Section

Row 1 (WS): K across.

Row 2 (RS): K2tog, K to last 2 sts, SSK. 2 sts dec.

Row 3: K across.

Rep Rows 2–3 13 more times. 22 sts.

Break C2, join C1.

Work Rows 2–3 nine times. 4 sts.

Next Row: K2tog, SSK. 2 sts.

Break yarn and pull through remaining sts.

Rep on opposite side to form final segment of larger square. Rep with all remaining Square As. 24 total Square Bs worked, 12 larger squares formed.

Prepare for Applying Border

Weave in ends, tying tog CO ends of the two Square As and the two Square Bs to close up middle of each bigger square. Block each larger square to 13.5" square.

Using Mattress Stitch seaming method and C1, sew squares tog in a rectangle three squares wide by four squares tall, making sure to line up squares so that Square A edges meet Square B edges. None of the sides being seamed tog should be the same colors as each other.

Throw Border

The border is joined to the throw as it is worked. Begin picking up sts along LH side of throw at bottom corner.

Side Border

With C4 and Crochet Cast On, CO 14 sts.

Row 1 (RS): K across.

Row 2 (WS): WYIF, Sl1 P-wise, WYIB, K to end.

Rows 3–28: Rep Rows 1–2 13 more times.

Row 29: With LH needle, PU st in bottom LH corner of throw, then K2tog (first st tog with PU st), K to end.

Row 30: WYIF, Sl1 P-wise, WYIB, K to end.

Row 31: With LH needle, PU edge st of next Garter ridge, then K2tog (first st tog with PU st), K to end.

Row 32: WYIF, Sl1 P-wise, WYIB, K to end.

Rows 33–34: Rep Rows 31–32.

Row 35: With LH needle, PU st in the space after the Garter ridge just joined, then K2tog (first st tog with PU st), K to end.

Row 36: WYIF, Sl1 P-wise, WYIB, K to end.

Rep Rows 31–36 until border reaches end of edge of throw. BO all sts.

Rep directions for Side Border along top, then again down RH side, then along bottom.

Sew BO edges of border sections to the sides of the strips next to them.

Throw Finishing

Weave in ends.

PILLOW DIRECTIONS

Make four Square As same as in Throw Directions.

Make four Square Bs, joining with Square As to make two larger squares as for Throw.

Block each larger square to 13.5" square.

Pillow Border

Border is joined to pillow as it is worked. Begin picking up sts along RH side of one square at bottom corner.

Side Border

With C4 and Crochet Cast On, CO 5 sts.

Row 1 (RS): K across.

Row 2 (WS): WYIF, Sl1 P-wise, WYIB, K to end.

Rows 3–12: Rep Rows 1–2 five more times.

Row 13: With LH needle, PU st in bottom LH corner of square, then K2tog (first st tog with PU st), K to end.

Row 14: WYIF, Sl1 P-wise, WYIB, K to end.

Row 15: With LH needle, PU edge st of next Garter ridge, then K2tog (first st tog with PU st), K to end.

Row 16: WYIF, Sl1 P-wise, WYIB, K to end.

Row 17–18: Rep Rows 15–16.

Row 19: With LH needle, PU st in the space after the Garter ridge just joined, then K2tog (first st tog with PU st), K to end.

Row 20: WYIF, Sl1 P-wise, WYIB, K to end.

Rep Rows 15–20 until border reaches end of edge of square. BO all sts.

Rep directions for Side Border along top, then again down RH side, then along bottom.

Sew BO edges of border sections to the sides of the strips next to them.

Rep for second square.

Pillow Finishing

Weave in ends.

Sew the two pieces tog around three edges with WSs tog.

Place over pillow form. Sew remaining edges tog.

Weave in any ends from seaming.

COLOR IT YOURSELF!

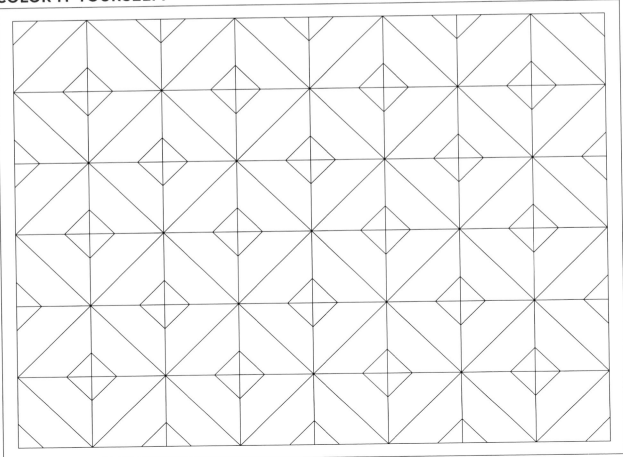

FLASH FORWARD

by Holli Yeoh

FINISHED MEASUREMENTS
48″ × 64″

YARN
Swish™ (worsted weight, 100% Fine Superwash Merino Wool; 110 yards/50g):
C1 White 24662, C2 Marble Heather 25153, 15 skeins each;
C3 Honey 26066, C4 Wonderland Heather 26067, C5 Conch 26068, C6 Peapod 25139, 1 skein each

NEEDLES
US 7 (4.5mm) straight or circular needles, or size to obtain gauge

NOTIONS
Yarn Needle
Locking Stitch Markers

GAUGE
18 sts and 40 rows = 4″ in Garter Stitch, blocked

For pattern support, contact info@holliyeoh.com

Flash Forward

Notes:

Pops of color and strong angles transform a simple checkerboard motif into a bold design full of movement. Customize the color scheme and elevate your room décor.

The color blocks are worked in long Garter Stitch strips, each joined to the one before it as the blanket grows, so there's no seaming and only one color in use at a time. Spit splice joins to minimize weaving in of ends. Simple increases and decreases create the chevrons.

Slip all stitches as if to purl unless otherwise noted.

Because RS and WS rows look the same in Garter Stitch, pin a locking stitch marker to the RS of your project to help differentiate the sides.

This blanket uses a modular technique called strip knitting. The blanket is constructed out of narrow strips worked on the bias, which are joined together as they are knit.

When joining strips, pick up the selvage st through both loops.

Each modular block is 28 rows / 14 Garter Stitch ridges and selvage loops.

It's recommended to check the stitch count occasionally; it's easy to accidentally miss or add a decrease or increase.

Assembly Diagram

Use assembly diagram as a guide for color placement. Assembly diagram is worked from right to left and bottom to top, beginning with Strip 1. Change colors as indicated using the Spit Splicing Two Colors method to minimize the number of ends to weave in.

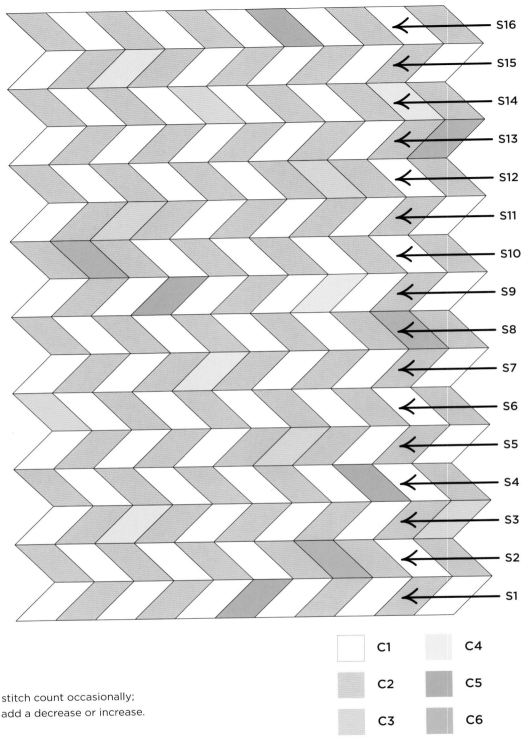

S16
S15
S14
S13
S12
S11
S10
S9
S8
S7
S6
S5
S4
S3
S2
S1

	C1		C4
	C2		C5
	C3		C6

Spit Splicing Two Colors

To minimize the number of ends to sew in, when joining a new color, use the spit splice method, even with superwash wool. It's important to break the yarn as opposed to cutting it with scissors; the feathery ends help camouflage the join.

K to end of last row of a color. Place a locking st M through working yarn immediately after last st worked. Undo the last 6–8 sts. Break yarn 2" beyond M. Take note of tail length from last st worked and how many sts remain to be worked in row. This will be the location to stop and break yarn and the measurement to use when joining new colors for future blocks.

Untwist last 4" of yarn tail and separate the plies. Remove half of the plies. Do the same with the new color. Cross the two ends (old and new colors) so they're perpendicular to one another, and fold tails back on themselves, overlapping unplied sections. Carefully hold all ends tog, wet yarn, and between the palms of your hands, briskly rub them in place until individual plies are felted tog. This completes the spit splice. There are approx 2" of felted old color followed by 2" of felted new color. When knitting resumes, join should land approx at end of row. There is no need to wait until join has dried before resuming knitting.

A tutorial for Spit Splicing Two Colors can be found at holliyeoh.com/spit-splicing-two-colours.

Right-Leaning Modular Strip Pattern
Row 1 (RS): KFB, K to last 3 sts, K2tog, Sl1 WYIF; with RH needle, insert tip through next selvage loop on previous strip as if to P, wrap yarn around needle P-Wise and pull loop through selvage loop to PU and P a new st; PSSO.
Row 2 (WS): Sl1 K-wise, K to last st, Sl1 WYIF.
Rep Rows 1–2 to desired length for pattern.

Left-Leaning Modular Strip Pattern
Row 1 (RS): K1, K2tog, K to last 2 sts, KFB, Sl1 WYIF; with RH needle, insert tip through next selvage loop on previous strip as if to P, wrap yarn around needle P-Wise and pull loop through selvage loop to PU and P a new st; PSSO.
Row 2 (WS): Sl1 K-wise, K to last st, Sl1 WYIF.
Rep Rows 1–2 to desired length for pattern.

K2tog Bind Off
*K2tog, transfer st just worked to LH needle; rep from * until all sts have been bound off.

DIRECTIONS

Strip 1
With C1, using Cabled Cast On method, CO 28 sts.
Row 1 (RS): K1, K2tog, K to last 2 sts, KFB, Sl1 WYIF.
Row 2 (WS): K to last st, Sl1 WYIF.
Rep Rows 1–2 twelve more times, ending with a WS row. 13 selvage loops. Break C1.
Using assembly diagram as a guide, join next color and work 28 rows (14 selvage loops) as established for each color in sequence, until eleven blocks of color have been worked, ending with a WS row.
Using K2tog Bind Off method, BO all sts.

Strip 2
With RS of previous strip facing, using C2, PU and K 1 st in lower-most CO st below first selvage loop on RH edge. Holding needle with single st in left hand, and using Cabled Cast On method, CO an additional 27 sts. 28 sts.
Work Right-Leaning Modular Strip Pattern for 26 rows, ending with a WS row. 13 selvage loops. Break C2.
Using assembly diagram, join next color and work 28 rows (14 selvage loops) as established for each color in sequence, until eleven blocks of color have been worked, ending with a WS row.
Using K2tog Bind Off method, BO all sts.

Strip 3
With RS of previous strip facing, using C3, PU and K 1 st in lower-most CO st below first selvage loop on RH edge. Holding needle with single st in left hand, and using Cabled Cast On method, CO an additional 27 sts. 28 sts.
Work Left-Leaning Modular Strip Pattern for 26 rows, ending with a WS row. 13 selvage loops. Break C3.
Using assembly diagram, join next color and work 28 rows (14 selvage loops) as established for each color in sequence, until eleven blocks of color have been worked, ending with a WS row.
Using K2tog Bind Off method, BO all sts.

Strips 4–16
Using assembly diagram as a guide for color placement, rep Strips 2–3, ending with a Strip 2.

Finishing
Weave in ends. Gently block to measurements, pinning out tips of chevrons for crisp, sharp angles.

FLOWER WAVES

by Adrienne Larsen

FINISHED MEASUREMENTS
36″ × 36″

YARN
Wool of the Andes™ Superwash
(worsted weight, 100% Superwash
Wool; 110 yards/50g):
C1 Clarity 26337, 3 skeins;
C2 Fjord Heather 26316, 6 skeins;
C3 Noble Heather 26301, 5 skeins;
C4 Aurora Heather 26308, 4 skeins

NEEDLES
US 10.5 (6.5mm) 24–32″ circular needles,
or size to obtain gauge

NOTIONS
Yarn Needle
Stitch Markers, 1 Removable

GAUGE
12 sts and 27 rows = 4″ in Garter Stitch
with two strands held together, blocked

For pattern support, contact adrienne.larsen@gmail.com

Flower Waves

Notes:

This blanket was an experiment with triangular entrelac and double stranding. The final design is reminiscent of a flower.

The triangles in this blanket are worked from the inside outward.

BT (Base Triangle; flat over 24 sts)
Rows 1–2: K2, turn.
Rows 3–4: K3, turn.
Rows 5–6: K4, turn.
Rows 7–8: K5, turn.
Rows 9–10: K6, turn.
Rows 11–12: K7, turn.
Rows 13–14: K8, turn.
Rows 15–16: K9, turn.
Rows 17–18: K10, turn.
Rows 19–20: K11, turn.
Rows 21–22: K12, turn.
Rows 23–24: K13, turn.
Rows 25–26: K14, turn.
Rows 27–28: K15, turn.
Rows 29–30: K16, turn.
Rows 31–32: K17, turn.
Rows 33–34: K18, turn.
Rows 35–36: K19, turn.
Rows 37–38: K20, turn.
Rows 39–40: K21, turn.
Rows 41–42: K22, turn.
Rows 43–44: K23, turn.
Row 45: K24.

ET (End Triangle; flat over 48 sts)
Row 1 (WS): K24.
Row 2 (RS): SSK, K21, SSK (with last st of previous triangle), turn. 2 sts dec.
Row 3: K23.
Row 4: SSK, K20, SSK, turn. 2 sts dec.
Row 5: K22.
Row 6: SSK, K19, SSK, turn. 2 sts dec.
Cont in this pattern, working 1 fewer st every other row until these final rows.
Row 44: SSK, SSK, turn.
Row 45: K2.
Row 46 (RS): SSK, SSK.
BO 1 st (leaving final st live).

JT (Joint Triangle; flat over 48 sts)
Row 1 (RS): K1, turn.
Row 2 (WS): K3tog, turn. 2 sts dec.
Row 3: K2, turn.
Row 4: K1, K2tog, turn. 1 st dec.
Row 5: K3, turn.
Row 6: K2, K2tog, turn. 1 st dec.
Row 7: K4, turn.

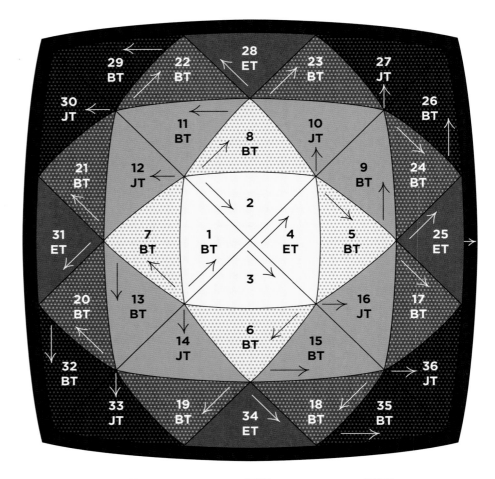

 C1 & C1
 C2 & C2   C3 & C3
 C1 & C2
 C2 & C3   C3 & C4

C4 & C4

Row 8: K3, K2tog, turn. 1 st dec.
Row 9: K5, turn.
Row 10: K4, K2tog, turn. 1 st dec.
Row 11: K6, turn.
Row 12: K5, K2tog, turn. 1 st dec.
Row 13: K7, turn.
Row 14: K6, K2tog, turn. 1 st dec.
Row 15: K8, turn.
Row 16: K7, K2tog, turn. 1 st dec.
Row 17: K9, turn.
Row 18: K8, K2tog, turn. 1 st dec.
Row 19: K10, turn.
Row 20: K9, K2tog, turn. 1 st dec.
Row 21: K11, turn.
Row 22: K10, K2tog, turn. 1 st dec.
Row 23: K12, turn.
Row 24: K11, K2tog, turn. 1 st dec.
Row 25: K13, turn,
Row 26: K12, K2tog, turn. 1 st dec.
Row 27: K14, turn.

Row 28: K13, K2tog, turn. 1 st dec.
Row 29: K15, turn.
Row 30: K14, K2tog, turn. 1 st dec.
Row 31: K16, turn.
Row 32: K15, K2tog, turn. 1 st dec.
Row 33: K17, turn.
Row 34: K16, K2tog, turn. 1 st dec.
Row 35: K18, turn.
Row 36: K17, K2tog, turn. 1 st dec.
Row 37: K19, turn.
Row 38: K18, K2tog, turn. 1 st dec.
Row 39: K20, turn.
Row 40: K19, K2tog, turn. 1 st dec.
Row 41: K21, turn.
Row 42: K20, K2tog, turn. 1 st dec.
Row 43: K22, turn.
Row 44: K21, K2tog, turn. 1 st dec.
Row 45: K23, turn.
Row 46: K22, K2tog, turn. 1 st dec.
Row 47 (RS): K24. Do not turn. 24 sts.

DIRECTIONS

Triangle 1
With two strands C1 held tog, CO 24 sts.
Work BT. For this triangle, odd number rows are RS.
Put a removable M into fabric to mark Triangle 1.

Triangle 2
Row 1 (WS): K2, turn.
Row 2 (RS): K2.
Row 3: KFB, SSK, turn.
Row 4: K3.
Row 5: KFB, K1, SSK, turn.
Row 6: K4.
Row 7: KFB, K2, SSK, turn.
Cont in this pattern, working 1 more st on each odd row, until completing the last row as follows.
Row 45 (WS): KFB, K21, SSK.
These 24 live sts will not be worked until Triangle 4.

Triangle 3
PU and P 24 sts along WS edge of Triangle 1.
Row 1 (RS): P2tog, P22, turn. 1 st dec.
Row 2 (WS): P23.
Row 3: P2tog, P21, turn. 1 st dec.
Row 4: P22.
Cont in this pattern; dec 1 st every other row, until completing the last row as follows.
Row 45 (RS): P2tog, do not turn.

Triangle 4
PU and K 23 sts along Triangle 3. Turn.
Work ET (Row 1 is worked over the just picked-up sts; this triangle will join to the live sts from Triangle 2).

Setup for Triangles 5–8
Break one strand C1. Join C2 to work with one strand C1 and one strand C2 held tog.
Next Row (RS): PU and K 23 sts along Triangle 2, PM, PU and K 24 sts along Triangle 1, PM, PU and K 24 sts along Triangle 3, PM, PU and K 24 sts along Triangle 4, PM, turn. 96 sts.

Triangle 5
Work BT, do not turn after last row. For this triangle and the following BTs through Triangle 8, odd number rows are WS.

Triangle 6
Work BT, do not turn after last row.

Triangle 7
Work BT, do not turn after last row.

Triangle 8
Work BT, do not turn after last row.

Triangle 9
Break C1. Join C2 to work with two strands C2 held tog.
PU and P 24 sts along WS of Triangle 5. Turn work.
Work BT, do not turn after last row. For this triangle and the following BTs through Triangle 15, odd number rows are RS.

Triangle 10
Work JT. Break yarn.

Triangle 11
PU and P 24 sts along WS of Triangle 8 edge. Turn work.
Work BT, do not turn after last row.

Triangle 12
Work JT. Break yarn.

Triangle 13
PU and P 24 sts along WS of Triangle 7 edge. Turn work.
Work BT, do not turn after last row.

Triangle 14
Work JT. Break yarn.

Triangle 15
PU and P 24 sts along WS of Triangle 6 edge. Turn work.
Work BT, do not turn after last row.

Triangle 16
Work JT.

Setup for Triangles 17–24
Break one strand C2. Join C3 to work with one strand C2 and one strand C3 held tog.
Next Row (RS): PU and K 24 sts along Triangle 9, PM, P24 across Triangle 10 sts, PM, PU and K 24 sts along Triangle 11, PM, P24 across Triangle 12 sts, PM, PU and K 24 sts along Triangle 13, PM, P24 across Triangle 14 sts, PM, PU and K 24 sts along Triangle 15, PM, P24 across Triangle 16 sts, PM, turn. 192 sts.

Triangle 17
Work BT, do not turn after last row. For this triangle and the following BTs through Triangle 24, odd number rows are WS.

Triangle 18

Work BT using sts from Triangle 15, do not turn after last row.

Triangle 19

Work BT using sts from Triangle 14, do not turn after last row.

Triangle 20

Work BT using sts from Triangle 13, do not turn after last row.

Triangle 21

Work BT using sts from Triangle 12, do not turn after last row.

Triangle 22

Work BT using sts from Triangle 11, do not turn after last row.

Triangle 23

Work BT using sts from Triangle 10, do not turn after last row.

Triangle 24

Work BT using sts from Triangle 9, do not turn after last row.

Triangle 25

Break C2. Join C3 to work with two strands C3 held tog.
PU and P 24 sts along WS of Triangle 17. Turn.
Work ET, starting with Row 2 (RS).
Break yarn and pull through final loop.

Triangle 26

Begin working with one strand C3 and one strand C4 held tog.
PU and P 24 sts along WS of Triangle 24. Turn.
Work BT, do not turn after last row. For this triangle and the following BTs through Triangle 35, odd number rows are RS.

Triangle 27

Work JT.

Triangle 28

Break C4. Join C3 to work with two strands C3 held tog.
PU and K 24 sts along Triangle 23. Turn.
Work ET. Break yarn and pull through final loop.

Triangle 29

Begin working with one strand C3 and one strand C4 held tog.
PU and P 24 sts along WS of Triangle 22. Turn.
Work BT, do not turn after last row.

Triangle 30

Work JT.

Triangle 31

Break C4. Join C3 to work with two strands C3 held tog.
PU and K 24 sts along Triangle 21. Turn.
Work ET. Break yarn and pull through final loop.

Triangle 32

Begin working with one strand C3 and one strand C4 held tog.
PU and P 24 sts along WS of Triangle 20. Turn.
Work BT, do not turn after last row.

Triangle 33

Work JT.

Triangle 34

Break C4. Join C3 to work with two strands C3 held tog.
PU and K 24 sts along Triangle 19. Turn.
Work ET. Break yarn and pull through final loop.

Triangle 35

Begin working with one strand C3 and one strand C4 held tog.
PU and P 24 sts along WS of Triangle 18. Turn.
Work BT, do not turn after last row.

Triangle 36

Work JT. Turn.
Final Row (WS): K24. Turn.

Edging

Break C3. Join C4 to work with two strands C4 held tog.
Rnd 1 (RS): M1, (K3, M1) eight times across Triangle 36, PU and K 33 sts across Triangle 25, PU and K 33 sts across Triangle 26, PM, M1P, (P3, M1P) eight times across Triangle 27, PU and K 33 sts across Triangle 28, PU and K 33 sts across Triangle 29, PM, M1P, (P3, M1P) eight times across Triangle 30, PU and K 33 sts across Triangle 31, PU and K 33 sts across Triangle 32, PM, M1P, (P3, M1P) eight times across Triangle 33, PU and K 33 sts across Triangle 34, PU and K 33 sts across Triangle 35, PM for BOR. 396 sts.
Rnd 2: P all.
Rnd 3: (KFB, K to 1 st before M, KFB, SM) four times.
8 sts inc.
Rep Rnds 2–3 two more times. 420 sts.
BO all sts P-wise, loosely.

Finishing

Weave in ends, wash, and block to measurements.

COLOR IT YOURSELF!

JOINERY

by Holli Yeoh

FINISHED MEASUREMENTS
48″ × 72″

YARN
Wool of the Andes™ Superwash
(worsted weight, 100% Superwash
Wool; 110 yards/50g): Fjord Heather
26316, 36 skeins

NEEDLES
US 7 (4.5mm) straight or circular
needles, plus 2 DPNs for optional border,
or size to obtain gauge

NOTIONS
Yarn Needle
Locking Stitch Markers
Stitch Holders or Scrap Yarn

GAUGE
18 sts and 32 rows = 4″ in Garter Stitch,
blocked

Joinery

Notes:

Modular joins become a design element in this textural, single-color blanket. Diagonal lines play across the surface to create an interesting knit and visually pleasing graphic that looks great on both sides, making the blanket reversible.

Worked entirely in Garter Stitch, narrow strips made on the bias are joined to the blanket as they're worked. The pattern is easy to memorize and can be knit almost entirely from the assembly diagram once the modules are mastered.

Slip all stitches as if to purl unless otherwise noted.

Although the blanket is reversible, RS and WS rows are indicated for clarity in the instructions. Because RS and WS rows look the same in Garter Stitch, pin a locking stitch marker to the RS of your project to help differentiate sides.

This blanket uses a modular technique called strip knitting. The blanket is constructed out of triangles and narrow strips worked on the bias, which are joined together as they are knit. When joining strips, pick up the selvage st through both loops.

Each modular unit is 48 rows, which equals 24 Garter Stitch ridges and selvage loops.

At the end of each modular unit, place a marker through the edge stitch on the RH edge with RS facing; this will make it easier to keep an accurate row count when joining a new module to the selvage loops. Check stitch count occasionally; it's easy to miss or add a decrease or increase accidentally.

The Center Decreasing Triangle (CDT) module has a right twist (RT) worked in the first row; this simply allows the stitches to lie flat as they transition over two preceding modules. Overall it looks better when the stitches are worked this way, but the right twist may also be omitted.

An applied I-Cord border (optional) creates a clean edge and coordinates particularly well with the joins on the WS. The I-Cord aids with the finishing process because most of the ends can be hidden in the center of the I-Cord. Weave in ends as Applied I-Cord is worked.

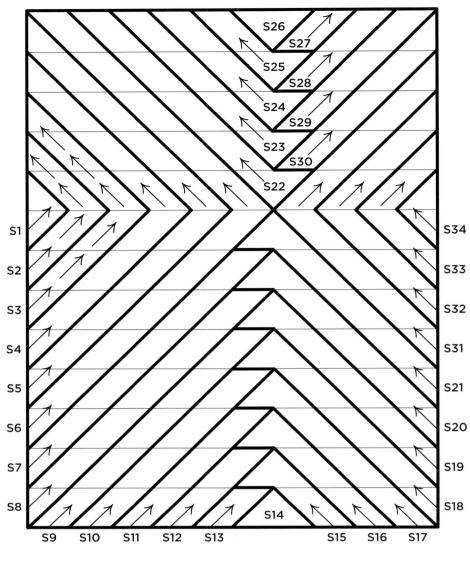

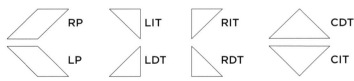

Assembly Diagram

Use the assembly diagram as a guide for module placement. Assembly diagram is worked from left side to right side, beginning with Section 1.

Cabled Cast On

Make a slip knot and place loop on LH needle. K1 without dropping old st from LH needle. Insert LH needle into front leg of new st and slip on to LH needle. 2 sts on LH needle. *Insert RH needle between first and second st on LH needle and K1 without dropping old st from LH needle. Sl new st on to LH needle. Rep from *.

RT (right twist, without a cable needle)

Knit into second st on needle, leaving sts on LH needle, then knit into first st on needle, sliding both sts off LH needle.

Spit Splicing

When possible, join yarn by spit splicing to tail of adjacent module; this is only possible when beginning Sections 9 and 23–30. Splice when joining a new ball to the end of an old ball. This works with wool, wool blends, and superwash wool. It's important to break yarn as opposed to cutting it with scissors; the feathery ends help camouflage the join.

Untwist last 2″ of tail and separate plies, remove half the plies, and do the same with new yarn. Lay remaining plies alongside one another, wet yarn between palms of hands, briskly rub them in place until individual plies are felted tog.

K2tog Bind Off

*K2tog, transfer st just worked to LH needle; rep from * until all sts have been bound off.

Applied I-Cord (worked over 5 sts, using two DPNs)

*With RS facing, slide sts to other end of needle. With yarn coming behind work from fifth st on needle, K4, Sl1 K-wise, YO, insert needle into selvage edge and PU and K 1 st. Pass 2 sts (YO st and Sl st) over last st. 5 sts. Rep from * working into every selvage loop and every CO or BO st.

Plain I-Cord (worked over 5 sts, using two DPNs)

*K5; without turning, slide sts to opposite end of needle to work RS, pull yarn tightly across from end of row; rep from *.

Non-Joining Modular Units

Right Increasing Triangle (RIT)

Begin with 2 sts.
Row 1 (RS): KFB, K to last st, WYIF Sl1. 1 st inc.
Row 2 and all WS Rows: K to last st, WYIF Sl1.
Rep Rows 1–2 20 more times, ending with a WS row. 23 sts; 21 selvage loops.
Work two rows even, maintaining slipped selvage sts.
Rep Rows 1–2 once more. 24 sts; 23 selvage loops.
Work two rows even, maintaining slipped selvage sts. 24 selvage loops.

Right Decreasing Triangle (RDT)

Begin with 24 sts.
Row 1 (RS): K1, K2tog, K to last st, WYIF Sl1. 1 st dec.
Row 2 and all WS Rows: K to last st, WYIF Sl1.
Row 3: K to last st, WYIF Sl1.
Rows 5–8: Rep Rows 1–4 once. 22 sts remain; 4 selvage loops.
Rep Rows 1–2 19 more times, ending with a WS row. 3 sts remain; 23 selvage loops.
Next RS Row: SSK, WYIF Sl1. 2 sts remain.
Next WS Row: K1, transfer st to LH needle, pass second st over st closest to needle tip. 1 st remains; 24 selvage loops. Break yarn and fasten off.

Joining Modular Units (listed alphabetically)

For all units, PU sts into the selvage loops evenly along adjacent modular unit to the next marked selvage loop.

JM (join module): WYIF Sl1. With RH needle, insert tip through next selvage loop on previous strip as if to purl, wrap yarn around needle P-wise and pull loop back through selvage loop, thus picking up and purling a new st, PSSO.

Center Decreasing Triangle (CDT)

Begin with 48 sts.
Row 1 (RS): K23, RT, K to last st, JM.
Row 2 (WS): Sl1 K-wise, K to last st, WYIF Sl1.
Row 3: K1, K2tog, K to last 3 sts, K2tog, JM. 2 sts dec.
Row 4: Rep Row 2.
Rep Rows 3–4 21 more times until 4 sts remain.
Next RS Row: K1, K2tog, JM. 3 sts remain.
Next WS Row: Sl1 K-wise, K1, WYIF Sl1.
Next Row: K3tog. 1 st remains; 24 selvage loops.
Break yarn and fasten off.

Center Increasing Triangle (CIT)

Begin with 3 sts.
Row 1 (RS): KFB, K1, JM. 4 sts.
Row 2 (WS): Sl1 K-wise, K to last st, WYIF Sl1.
Row 3: KFB, K to last 2 sts, KFB, JM. 2 sts inc.
Row 4: Rep Row 2.
Rep Rows 3–4 21 more times. 48 sts; 23 selvage loops.
Next RS Row: K to last st, WYIF Sl1, JM.
Next WS Row: Sl1 K-wise, K23, (all in same st: M1 leaving lifted st on LH needle, YO, K1 into lifted st), K to last st, WYIF Sl1. 51 sts; 24 selvage loops.

Left Decreasing Triangle (LDT)

Begin with 24 sts.
Row 1 (RS): K to last 3 sts, K2tog, WYIF Sl1. 1 st dec.
Row 2 and all WS Rows: K to last st, WYIF Sl1.
Row 3: K to last st, WYIF Sl1.
Rows 5–8: Rep Rows 1–4 once.
Rep Rows 1–2 19 more times, ending with a WS row. 3 sts remain; 23 selvage loops.
Next RS Row: SSK, WYIF Sl1. 2 sts remain.
Next WS Row: K1, transfer st to LH needle, pass second st over st closest to needle tip. 1 st remains; 24 selvage loops. Break yarn and fasten off.

Left Increasing Triangle (LIT)

Begin with 2 sts.
Row 1 (RS): KFB, JM.
Row 2 and all WS Rows: Sl1 K-wise, K to last st, WYIF Sl1.
Row 3: K to last 2 sts, KFB, JM.
Rep Rows 3–4 19 more times, ending with a WS row. 23 sts; 21 selvage loops.
Work two rows even, maintaining slipped selvage sts and join at end of RS row.
Rep Rows 3–4 once more. 24 sts; 23 selvage loops.
Work two rows even, maintaining slipped selvage sts and join at end of RS row. 24 selvage loops.

Left-Leaning Parallelogram (LP)

Row 1 (RS): K1, K2tog, K to last 2 sts, KFB, JM.
Row 2 (WS): Sl1 K-wise, K to last st, WYIF Sl1.
Rep Rows 1–2 23 more times, ending with a WS row. 24 selvage loops.

Right-Leaning Parallelogram (RP)
Row 1 (RS): KFB, K to last 3 sts, K2tog, JM.
Row 2 (WS): Sl1 K-wise, K to last st, WYIF Sl1.
Rep Rows 1–2 23 more times, ending with a WS row.
24 selvage loops.

DIRECTIONS

Section 1
CO 2 sts.
Work one RIT, PM in last selvage loop on RH edge of module (with RS facing). 24 sts; 24 selvage loops.
Work one RDT.

Section 2
CO 2 sts.
Work one RIT, PM in last selvage loop on RH edge. 24 sts; 24 selvage loops.
With RS of previous section facing, work one RP joining it to right edge of previous section, beginning at first row (see assembly diagram for placement). PM in last selvage loop of module.
Work one LP. PM at end of module.
Work one RDT.

Sections 3, 4 & 5
Using assembly diagram as a guide, rep Section 2 working RP(s) and LP(s) as indicated, PM at end of each module.

Section 6
Rep Section 3 to last LP, ending with a WS row.
Using K2tog Bind Off method, BO all sts.

Section 7
Work as for Section 3, ending with WS row of final RP as shown on assembly diagram.
Break yarn and transfer sts to st holder or scrap yarn.

Section 8
Rep Section 7.

Section 9
With RS of previous section facing, PU and K 1 st in lower-most CO st below first selvage loop on RH edge. Holding needle with single st in LH, and using Cabled Cast On method, CO an additional 23 sts. 24 sts.
Work RP. PM in last selvage loop of module.
Using assembly diagram as a guide, work remaining RPs as indicated, ending with a WS row. PM at end of each module.
Break yarn and transfer sts to st holder or scrap yarn.

Sections 10, 11, 12 & 13
Work as for Section 9.

Section 14
With RS of previous section facing, PU and K 1 st in lower-most CO st below first selvage loop on RH edge. Holding needle with single st in LH, and using Cabled Cast On method, CO an additional 47 sts. 48 sts.
Row 1 (RS): K to last st, JM.
Work CDT from Row 2 to end.

Section 15
With RS of previous section facing, PU and K 1 st in lower-most CO st below first selvage loop on RH edge. Holding needle with single st in LH, and using Cabled Cast On method, CO an additional 23 sts. 24 sts.
Using assembly diagram as a guide, work LP(s) as indicated, ending with second to last row of final LP. PM at end of each module.
With WS facing, transfer adjacent section sts from holder to an empty needle, then work final row of LP onto same needle as held sts. 48 sts.
Work CDT.

Sections 16 & 17
Rep Section 15.

Section 18
With RS of previous section facing, PU and K 1 st in lower-most CO st below first selvage loop on RH edge. Holding needle with single st in LH, and using Cabled Cast On method, CO 1 st. 2 sts.
Work LIT. PM in last selvage loop of module. 24 sts.
Work as for Section 15 once the LPs begin.

Sections 19 & 20
With RS of previous section facing, PU and K 1 st in marked selvage loop of LIT (refer to assembly diagram). Holding needle with single st in LH, and using Cabled Cast On method, CO 1 st. 2 sts.
Work as for Section 18 beginning with LIT.

Section 21
Work as for Section 18 until 3 sts remain, ending with a WS row. Do not break yarn.

Section 22
Work CIT. PM in last selvage loop of module. 51 sts. Break yarn.
Transfer first 27 sts to st holder or scrap yarn. Leave remaining sts on needle.
With RS facing, rejoin yarn mid-row and work remaining 24 sts on needle as follows.
Using assembly diagram as a guide, work LP(s) as indicated, ending with a WS row. PM at end of each module, including last module.
Using K2tog Bind Off method, BO all sts.

Sections 23, 24 & 25
With RS facing, transfer last 3 sts from Sections 22, 23, 24 holder (respectively) to needle.
Join yarn. Work as for Section 22.

Section 26
Join yarn. Work CIT to last 2 rows. 48 sts; 23 selvage loops.
Work two rows even, maintaining slipped selvage sts and join at end of RS row. PM in last selvage loop of module.
Using K2tog Bind Off method, BO all sts.

Section 27
Using assembly diagram as a guide, slide sts from Section 25 holder (closest to base of previous section) to needle. 24 sts.
With RS facing, rejoin yarn.

Using assembly diagram as a guide, work RP(s) as indicated, ending with a WS row. PM at end of each module, including last module.
Using K2tog Bind Off method, BO all sts.

Sections 28 & 29
Work as for Section 27, using held sts from Sections 24 and 23, respectively.

Section 30
Using held sts from Section 22, work as for Section 27 to end of RPs.
Work LDT.

Section 31
With RS of Section 21 facing, PU and K 1 st in lower-most selvage loop on RH edge. Holding needle with single st in LH, and using Cabled Cast On method, CO 1 st. 2 sts.
Work LIT. PM in last selvage loop of module. 24 sts.
Using assembly diagram as guide, work LP(s) and RP(s) as indicated. PM at end of each module.
Work LDT.

Sections 32 & 33
Work as for Section 31.

Section 34
With RS of previous section facing, PU and K 1 st in marked selvage loop of LIT (refer to assembly diagram). Holding needle with single st in LH, and using Cabled Cast On method, CO 1 st. 2 sts.
Work LIT. PM in last selvage loop of module. 24 sts; 24 selvage loops.
Work LDT; do not break yarn or fasten off. 1 st.

Finishing
Border (optional)
See Notes for advice about working I-Cord.
Change to two DPNs.
With RS of Section 34 facing, hold needle with single st in left hand and using Backward Loop Cast On method, CO 4 sts. 5 sts.
*Work Applied I-Cord to next corner. Work 3 rnds of Plain I-Cord. Rep from * three more times. Work Applied I-Cord to beginning of I-Cord. Break yarn leaving a 12″ tail and graft ends tog.

Final Finishing
Weave in ends. Gently block to measurements, pinning out corners for crisp, sharp angles.

COLOR IT YOURSELF!

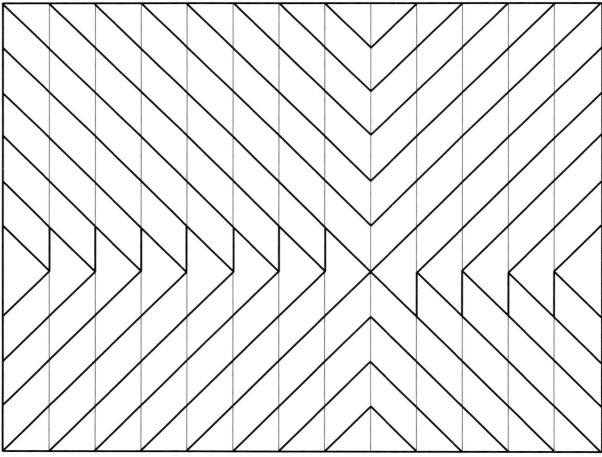

OUTLINE

by Joy Geib Doss for the Knit Picks Design Team

FINISHED MEASUREMENTS
51″ × 64″

YARN
Mighty Stitch™ (bulky weight, 80% Acrylic, 20% Superwash Wool; 136 yards/100g): C1 Sky 27158, C2 Silver 27157, 6 skeins each; C3 White 27160, 7 skeins

NEEDLES
US 10.5 (6.5mm) 24″ and 40″ circular needles, or size to obtain gauge
Size 3 (3.25mm) 32″ or longer circular needles
Size 15 (10mm) circular, straight, or DPNs

NOTIONS
Yarn Needle
Scrap Yarn (48 yards smooth yarn in a contrasting color, cut into 1-yard lengths)

GAUGE
10.5 sts and 21 rows = 4″ in Garter Stitch, blocked (gauge is not crucial, but it will affect finished size and yardage requirements)
Note: This is a very loose, drapey gauge in this yarn; if you'd prefer a denser gauge, either substitute a heavier yarn, or go down in needle size for a tighter gauge and a smaller finished size.

For pattern support, contact customerservice@knitpicks.com

Outline

Notes:

This twist on a classic log cabin style afghan features outlines around each bold color block and offers two different blanket configurations.

Great for warm-weather knitting, each square is made separately and then they are all joined together, minimizing lap-warmth. This pattern is worked entirely in Garter Stitch.

When rotating work, always turn piece one quarter turn, unless otherwise indicated.

Detailed diagrams for all squares are included at the end of the pattern in case some extra visual help is needed.

Choose assembly Option 1 or Option 2 before starting, as this choice will determine how Square A is worked. Squares B and C are worked the same for both options.

Always use middle-size needles (which obtain gauge) unless otherwise noted; these will be called the *main needles*.

DIRECTIONS

Square A (make four the same)

Block 1

This block is the same for Options 1 and 2.
With C3, CO 7 sts with a Long Tail Cast On.
Knit 15 rows.
Break C3.

Block 2

Join C1 and knit 14 rows.
Break C1 and put sts on scrap yarn to hold.
Option 1: With RS facing, rotate work counterclockwise.
Option 2: With RS facing, rotate work clockwise.

Block 3

Insert size 3 needle from left to right through top of each ridge—in Option 1 that will be 7 ridges of C1, then 8 ridges of C3; in Option 2 that will be 8 ridges of C3, then 7 ridges of C1. 15 sts.
With C3 and main needles, knit two rows, then break C3.
Join C2 and knit 14 rows.
Break C2 and put sts on scrap yarn.
Option 1: With RS facing, rotate work counterclockwise.
Option 2: With RS facing, rotate work clockwise.

Block 4

Option 1: With main needles and C3, PU and K 1 st in each CO st (total of 7). Insert size 3 needle from left to right through top of the 7 C2 ridges and 1 C3 ridge, then knit across these ridges. 15 sts.
Option 2: Insert size 3 needle from left to right through top of the 1 C3 ridge and 7 C2 ridges and knit across these ridges with C3 and main needles. Continuing with C3, PU and K 7 sts along CO edge. 15 sts.
All Options: Knit one row (WS row), then break C3.
Join C2 and knit 14 rows.

Option 1

C1

C2

C3

Option 2

Break C2 and put sts on scrap yarn.
Option 1: With RS facing, rotate work counterclockwise.
Option 2: With RS facing, rotate work clockwise.

Block 5

Insert size 3 needle from left to right through top of each ridge: 7 ridges in C1 or C2, 9 ridges in C3, and 7 ridges in C2 or C1; 23 ridges total.

With C3 and main needles, knit two rows, then break C3.

Join C1 and knit 14 rows.

Break C1 and put sts on scrap yarn.

Option 1: With RS facing, rotate work counterclockwise.

Option 2: With RS facing, rotate work clockwise.

Block 6

Insert size 3 needle from left to right through top of first 8 ridges (7 in C1 or C2 and 1 in C3), Sl the 7 sts from scrap yarn onto needle, then insert needle through top of last 8 ridges (1 in C3 and 7 in C2 or C1); total of 23 ridges and sts on needle.

With C3 and main needles, knit two rows, then break C3.

Join C1 and knit 14 rows.

Break C1 and put sts on scrap yarn.

Option 1: With RS facing, rotate work counterclockwise.

Option 2: With RS facing, rotate work clockwise.

Block 7

Insert size 3 needle from left to right through top of first 8 ridges (7 in C1 or C2 and 1 in C3), Sl the 15 sts from scrap yarn onto needle, then insert needle through top of last 8 ridges (1 in C3 and 7 in C2 or C1); total of 31 ridges and sts on needle.

With C3 and main needles, knit two rows, then break C3.

Join C2 and knit 14 rows.

Break C2 and put sts on scrap yarn.

Option 1: With RS facing, rotate work counterclockwise.

Option 2: With RS facing, rotate work clockwise.

Block 8

Work as for Block 7.

Block 9

Insert size 3 needle from left to right through top of first 8 ridges (7 in C1 or C2 and 1 in C3), Sl the 23 sts from scrap yarn onto needle, then insert needle through top of last 8 ridges (1 in C3 and 7 in C2 or C1); total of 39 ridges and sts on needle.

With C3 and main needles, knit two rows, then break C3.

Join C1 and knit 14 rows.

Break C1. Do not rotate.

Block 10

With RS facing, join C3 and knit four rows.

Break C3 leaving 48″ tail and put sts on scrap yarn.

With RS facing, rotate work one half turn.

Block 11

Option 1: Across top from left to right, Sl the 31 sts from scrap yarn onto size 3 needle, then insert needle through top of last 8 ridges (1 in C3 and 7 in C2); total of 39 ridges and sts on needle.

Option 2: Insert size 3 needle from left to right through top of first 8 ridges (7 in C2 and 1 in C3), then Sl the 31 sts from scrap yarn onto needle; total of 39 ridges and sts on needle.

All Options: With C3 and main needles, knit four rows.

Break C3 leaving 48″ tail and put sts on scrap yarn.

Finishing Square A

Weave in ends, except for 48″ tails.

Square B (make four the same)

Work entirely as for Square A, except:

For both assembly options, use **Option 2** instructions.

Do not leave a 48″ tail for Block 10.

Do not work Block 11 at all.

Square C (make four the same)

Work entirely as for Square A, except:

For both assembly options, use **Option 2** instructions.

At end of Block 9, put sts on scrap yarn.

Do not work Block 10 at all.

After Block 9, rotate work one half turn, then work Block 11, but do not leave a 48″ tail.

Join Squares

Join one each of Squares A, B, and C to make a strip (make four strips), as follows.

Select a Square B; put Block 10 sts from scrap yarn onto size 3 needle.

Select a Square A.

Option 1: Put Block 10 sts from scrap yarn onto main needles.

Option 2: Put Block 11 sts from scrap yarn onto main needles.

With RSs of the two squares facing each other and needles parallel with 48″ tail to the right, use other end of main needles in right hand to 3-Needle Bind Off all sts with tail. If seam is too tight, use larger needle to work BO. Break yarn.

Select a Square C; put Block 11 sts from scrap yarn onto size 3 needle.

Option 1: Using Square A from above step, put Block 11 sts from scrap yarn onto main needle.

Option 2: Using Square A from above step, put Block 10 sts from scrap yarn onto main needle.

With RSs of the two squares facing each other and needles parallel with 48″ tail to the right, use other end of main needles in right hand to 3-Needle Bind Off all sts with tail. If seam is too tight, use larger needle to work BO. Break yarn.

Join Four Strips

Lay out four strips as per assembly diagram—note that for Option 1, second and bottom strips are rotated 180 degrees.

Select two strips to seam. With size 3 needle and RS facing, PU each ridge and each st from scrap yarn along one of the sides to be seamed; 125 total ridges and sts. In picking up ridges, any block in C1 or C2 will be 7 ridges, C3 will either be 1 ridge or 4. The sections of C3 with 4 ridges include a seam—PU 2 ridges on either side of seam.

With C3 and main needles, knit four rows (starting with a RS row). Break C3 and put sts on scrap yarn (or hold on spare circular needle cable).

Rep that process for the side that will be joined with the side just completed, except do not break yarn, and leave sts on needles.

Put sts from scrap yarn (or held on cable) from first side onto size 3 needles. With RSs of the two strips facing each other and needles parallel with attached working yarn to the right, use other end of main needles in the right hand to 3-Needle Bind Off all sts. If seam is too tight, use larger needle to work BO. Break yarn.

Rep process for remaining two joins.

Border

Side Borders

Along a four-square side, with size 3 needle and RS facing, PU each ridge and each st from scrap yarn; 168 sts and ridges on needle. In picking up ridges, any block in C1 or C2 will be 7 ridges, C3 will either be 1 ridge or 4. The sections of C3 with 4 ridges include a seam—PU 2 ridges on either side of seam.

With C3 and main needles, knit eight rows (starting with a RS row).

Break C3 and put sts on scrap yarn.

Rep for other four-square side.

Top & Bottom Borders

Along a three-square side, with size 3 needle and RS facing, PU each ridge and each st from scrap yarn; 134 sts and ridges on needle. In picking up ridges, any block in C1 or C2 will be 7 ridges, C3 will either be 1 ridge or 4. The two inner sections of C3 with 4 ridges include a seam—PU 2 ridges on either side of seam.

With C3 and main needles, knit eight rows (starting with a RS row).

Break C3 and put sts on scrap yarn.

Rep for other three-square side, but leave sts on main needles and do not break yarn.

Bind Off Edge

Turn so RS is facing. With largest needle in right hand, BO all sts across needle. Insert size 3 needle into top of the 4 ridges on the next side and BO, then insert size 3 needle into sts from scrap yarn on this side and BO. Cont to BO ridges and sts from scrap yarn until BO goes all the way around throw.

Finishing

Break yarn, and weave in all remaining ends.
Block as desired.

Square A Option 1

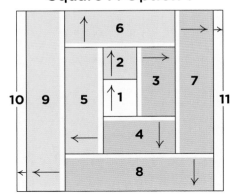

Square A Option 2

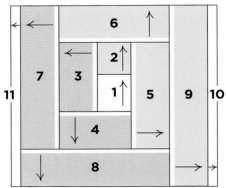

Square B

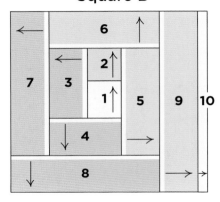

Square C

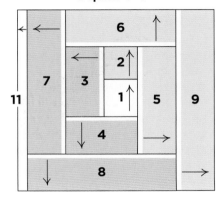

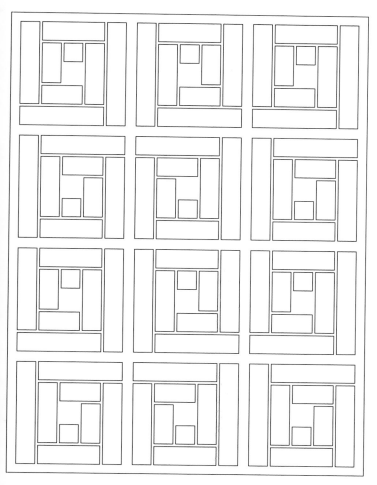

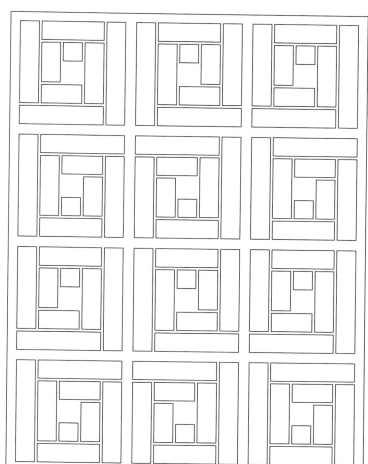

COLOR IT YOURSELF!

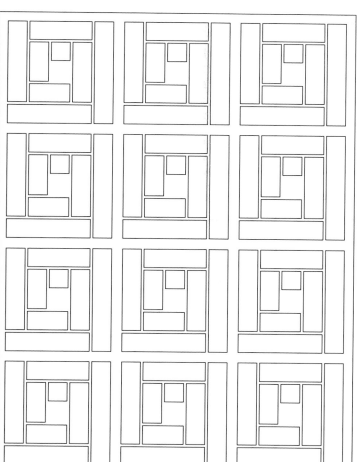

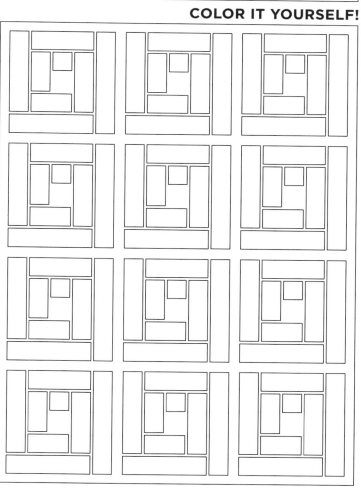

PINWHEELS FOR BILLY

by Suzanne Ross

FINISHED MEASUREMENTS

40″ × 40″ (9.5″ each individual square)

YARN

Brava™ (worsted weight, 100%
Premium Acrylic; 218 yards/100g):
MC White 28455, 4 skeins;
C1 Sky 28451, C2 Celestial 28418,
2 skeins each;
C3 Solstice Heather 28452, C4
Eggplant 28430, 1 skein each

NEEDLES

US 8 (5mm) straight or circular needles,
plus 32″ (or longer) circular needles for
borders, or size to obtain gauge

NOTIONS

Yarn Needle

GAUGE

18 sts and 36 rows = 4″ in Garter Stitch,
blocked

For pattern support, contact suzanneross22@yahoo.com

Pinwheels for Billy

Notes:

Named for a child who loves the way a pinwheel blows in the wind, Pinwheels for Billy is a knitted adaptation of a quilt design.

It is made with 16 squares knit in Garter Stitch, with simple decreases in a modular technique that makes assembly very easy. The afghan is finished with a Garter Stitch border.

DIRECTIONS

Squares
(make 16 the same)
Section A
With MC, CO 28 sts.
Row 1 (RS): K across.
Row 2 (WS): K across.
Row 3: K to last 3 sts, K2tog, K1. 1 st dec.
Row 4: K across.
Rows 5–52: Rep Rows 3–4. 3 sts.
Row 53: K2tog, K1. 2 sts.
Row 54: K2.
Row 55: K2tog. 1 st.
Break MC.

Section B
With RS facing, using C1, PU and K 28 sts along shorter, straight side of Section A. PU row is counted as Row 1.
Row 2 (WS): K across.
Row 3 (RS): K to last 3 sts, K2tog, K1. 1 st dec.
Row 4: K across.
Rows 5–10: Rep Rows 3–4 three more times. 24 sts. Break C1, join C2.
Rows 11–22: Rep Rows 3–4 six more times. 18 sts. Break C2, join C3.
Rows 23–36: Rep Rows 3–4 seven more times. 11 sts. Break C3, join C4.
Rows 37–52: Rep Rows 3–4 eight more times. 3 sts.
Row 53: K2tog, K1. 2 sts.
Row 54: K2.
Row 55: K2tog. 1 st.
Break C4.

Section C
With RS facing, using MC, PU and K 28 sts along shorter, straight side of Section B. PU row is counted as Row 1. Work Rows 2–55 as for Section A.

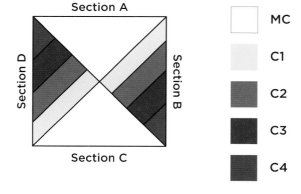

Section A
Section D
Section B
Section C

	MC
	C1
	C2
	C3
	C4

Section D
With RS facing, using C1, PU and K 28 sts along shorter, straight side of Section C. PU row is counted as Row 1. Work Rows 2–55 as for Section B.

Complete Square
Seam sides of Sections A and D tog to form square.

Finishing

Weave in ends, block squares, and assemble according to diagram.

Border

First Side (choose any side of blanket; this is the top edge in assembly diagram)

Using C2 and circular needle, with RS facing, PU and K 160 sts along one edge (40 sts along edge of each square).
Knit five rows.
BO all sts, leaving last st on RH needle.

Second Side

Rotate blanket a quarter-turn clockwise.
PU and K 163 sts along second edge—164 sts total (1 st from previous side, 3 sts along edge of previous side, and 40 sts along edge of each square).
Knit five rows.
BO all sts, leaving last st on RH needle.

Third Side

Work as for Second Side.

Fourth Side

PU and K 167 sts along last edge—168 sts total (1 st from previous side, 3 sts along edge of Third Side, 40 sts along edge of each square, and 4 sts along edge of First Side).
Knit five rows.
BO all sts.

Weave in remaining ends, block.

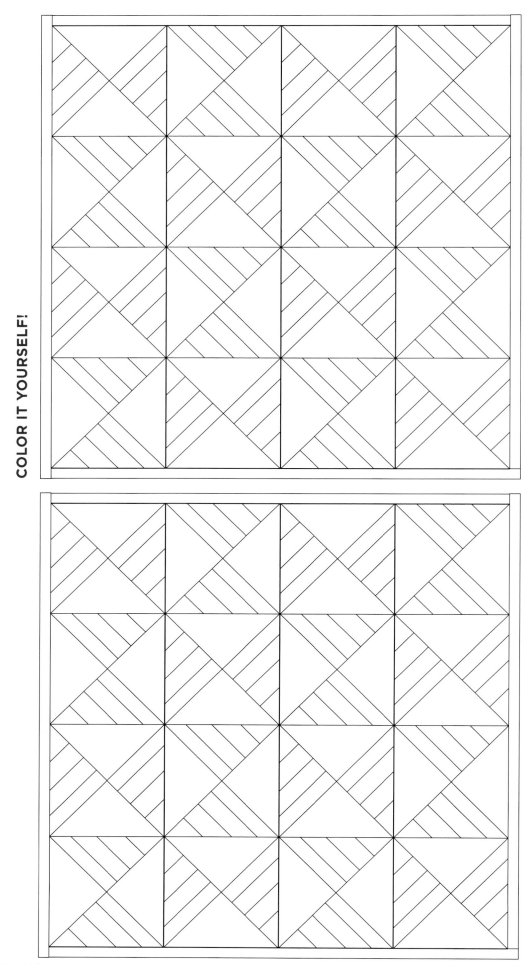

RAINFLAKE

by Mary Hull

FINISHED MEASUREMENTS

48 (54, 89)" × 53 (89, 90)" for
Square (Rectangular, Queen) sizes
Sample is Square size

YARN

Swish™ (DK weight, 100% Fine
Superwash Merino Wool; 123 yards/50g):
MC Dove Heather 24956, 9 (16, 26) skeins;
C1 Serrano 24632, 4 (7, 10) skeins;
C2 Allspice 25579, 0 (0, 6) skeins;
C3 Clementine 27224, 3 (6, 5) skeins;
C4 Honey 26061, 3 (5, 9) skeins;
C5 Peapod 24951, 2 (4, 4) skeins;
C6 Forest Heather 24307, 0 (0, 3) skeins;
C7 Marina 25578, 2 (3, 5) skeins;
C8 Gulfstream 24957, 2 (2, 2) skeins;
C9 Amethyst Heather 24310, 1 (2, 2) skeins;
C10 Indigo Heather 24954, 0 (1, 2) skeins

NEEDLES

US 7 (4.5mm) DPNs or 16" circular
needles or two 24" circular needles
for two circulars technique or 32" or
longer circular needles for Magic Loop
technique, or size to obtain gauge

NOTIONS

Yarn Needle
1 Stitch Marker

GAUGE

21 sts and 30 rows = 4" in Stockinette
Stitch, blocked (gauge is not crucial,
but it will affect finished size and
yardage requirements)
One finished Hexagon = 6" from side
to side, 6.75" from corner to opposite
corner

For pattern support, contact kinoknits@gmail.com

Rainflake

Notes:

The Rainflake Throw features a rainbow of hexagons with snowflake-like texture. The modular construction means it's easy to make blankets of different sizes and color configurations.

Each hexagon is knit in the round from the outside in. Avoid seaming by picking up and adding each hexagon modularly, or knit each hexagon individually and sew them together later for a more portable project. A hybrid approach is also possible, creating large modular sections that can be sewn together at the end.

If choosing to make each Hexagon individually and seam together at the end, start with the *Setup for Individual Hexagon* instructions for each one. The following number of Hexagons in each color will be needed for Square (Rectangular, Queen) sized blankets:

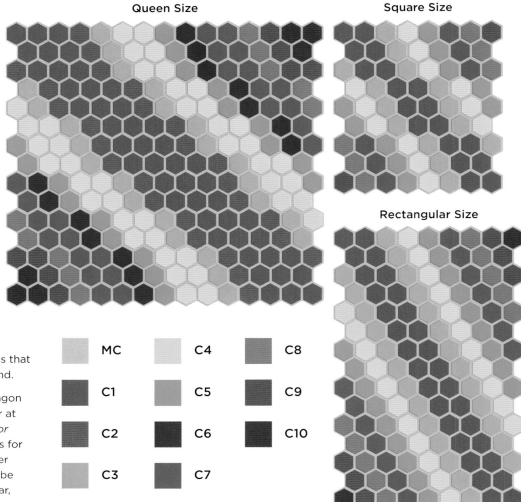

Queen Size

Square Size

Rectangular Size

MC	C4	C8
C1	C5	C9
C2	C6	C10
C3	C7	

C1	18 (30, 46)	**C6**	0 (0, 14)
C2	0 (0, 26)	**C7**	6 (10, 10)
C3	14 (26, 24)	**C8**	6 (6, 8)
C4	12 (22, 42)	**C9**	2 (6, 8)
C5	10 (18, 18)	**C10**	0 (2, 6)

If seaming, use Mattress Stitch to seam the hexagons together according to the appropriate diagram, weaving in ends at the same time.

If working modularly, start with *Setup for Individual Hexagon* and make the first hexagon using MC and C1, the top left hexagon of the throw. Then, using the diagram for the correct size, add hexagons in the appropriate colors by following the directions for *Setup to Join to One Hexagon* or *Setup to Join to Two Hexagons*, as needed. The number of overall Hexagons in each color will be the same as shown above.

DIRECTIONS

Setup for Individual Hexagon

Using MC, loosely CO 108 sts.
Join to work in the rnd, being careful not to twist sts.
PM for BOR.
Proceed to *Standard Hexagon* instructions.

Setup to Join to One Hexagon

With RS facing, find center of one edge of original hexagon, directly out from center knit spine. Starting from this point, use MC to PU and K 9 sts to corner of original hexagon. (Photo A)

Turn work and, using Cabled Cast On, CO 90 sts. 99 sts total. (Photo B)

Turn work and, being careful not to twist sts, PU and K 9 sts from beginning of same edge on original hexagon to original PU point. 108 sts total. (Photo C)

PM for BOR. Proceed to *Standard Hexagon* instructions.

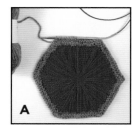

A

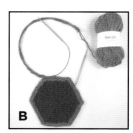

B

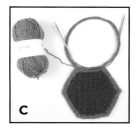

C

Setup to Join to Two Hexagons

Orient original two hexagons so that joining edge is facing up. With RS facing and starting in center of straight edge of hexagon on the right, directly out from center knit spine, use MC to PU and K 9 sts to corner between two original hexagons. (Photo D)

PU and K 18 sts along edge of second hexagon. 27 sts total. (Photo E)

Turn work and, using Cabled Cast On, CO 72 sts. 99 sts total. (Photo F)

Turn work and, being careful not to twist sts, PU and K 9 sts from beginning of same edge on original hexagon to original PU point. 108 sts total. (Photo G)

PM for BOR. Proceed to *Standard Hexagon* instructions.

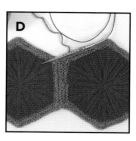

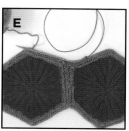

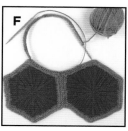

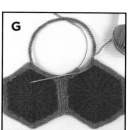

Standard Hexagon

Rnds 1–4 are worked in MC.
Rnd 1: P all.
Rnd 2: (K8, CDD, K7) six times. 96 sts.
Rnd 3: P all.
Rnd 4: K all.
Break MC, leaving approx 6" tail to weave in later.
Switch to color needed, C1 through C10.
Rnd 5: (K7, CDD, K6) six times. 84 sts.
Rnds 6–7: (K1, P2, K1, P2, K3, P2, K1, P2) six times.
Rnd 8: (K1, P2, K1, P2, CDD, P2, K1, P2) six times. 72 sts.
Rnds 9–10: (K1, P2) 24 times.
Rnd 11: (K1, P2, K1, P1, CDD, P1, K1, P2) six times. 60 sts.
Rnds 12–13: (K1, P2, K1, P1, K1, P1, K1, P2) six times.
Rnd 14: (K1, P2, K1, CDD, K1, P2) six times. 48 sts.
Rnds 15–16: (K1, P2, K3, P2) six times.
Rnd 17: (K1, P2, CDD, P2) six times. 36 sts.
Rnd 18: (K1, P2) twelve times.
Rnd 19: (K1, P1, CDD, P1) six times. 24 sts.
Rnd 20: (K1, P1) twelve times.
Rnd 21: (K1, CDD) six times. 12 sts.
Rnd 22: (K2tog) six times. 6 sts.
Break color yarn, leaving approx 6" tail. Bring tail through remaining 6 sts and pull tight.

Finishing

Once all hexagons are knit and, if necessary, seamed tog using MC, weave in all ends, wash, and block.

COLOR IT YOURSELF!

SQUARED

by Hope Vickman

FINISHED MEASUREMENTS

48 (28.75, 16.75)″ × 57.5 (38.5, 16.75)″
for Throw (Baby Blanket, Pillow)
(Pillow is 18″ × 18″ when stretched
over pillow form)
Sample is Throw size

YARN

Chroma™ (worsted weight, 70%
Superwash Wool, 30% Nylon; 198
yards/100g):
MC Bare 25266, 14 (6, 2) balls;
CC Pixie 28050, 5 (2, 1) balls

NEEDLES

US 7 (4.5mm) DPNs, 16″, 24″, and 32″
circular needles (32″ needed for Pillow
only), or size to obtain gauge

NOTIONS

Yarn Needle
3 Stitch Markers
1 Unique, Removable Stitch Marker
Scrap Yarn (5 yards)
For Pillow: 18″ Foam Pillow Insert

GAUGE

20 sts and 40 rows = 4″ in Garter Stitch,
blocked

For pattern support, contact hopefullyknitting@gmail.com

Squared

Notes:

Ever-growing colorful squares nestled in a neutral background create a geometric blanket that is both visually captivating and interesting to knit. Its simplicity and beauty will make it a welcome addition to any home.

Each square is worked individually in the round from the center out. Squares are joined to each other using 3-Needle Bind Off seams. See specific instructions for working the 3-Needle Bind Off for each square at the end of the pattern, upon completion of each square.

3NBO = Work 3-Needle Bind Off.

RM = Remove stitch marker.

SY = One piece of scrap yarn.

DIRECTIONS

Row 1 Squares (make five, for Throw only)
With CC and DPNs, CO 4 sts onto one DPN.
Setup Row: (KFB) four times. 8 sts. Arrange sts so there are 2 sts on each of four DPNs, join to work in the rnd, being careful not to twist sts.
Rnd 1: KFB twice on each DPN. 16 sts, 4 per DPN. Place removable M through st below first DPN for BOR.
Rnd 2: P all.
Rnd 3: (KFB, K to last st on DPN, KFB) four times. 8 sts inc.
Rnds 4–18: Rep Rnds 2–3 seven more times, then Rnd 2 once more. 80 sts.

Rnd 19: Using 16″ circular needle, (KFB, K to last st on DPN, KFB, PM) four times. Last M placed should be unique to denote BOR. 88 sts, 22 between Ms.
Rnd 20: P all.
Rnd 21: (KFB, K to 1 st before M, KFB, SM) four times. 8 sts inc.
Rnds 22–34: Rep Rnds 20–21 six more times, then Rnd 20 once more. 144 sts.

Rnd 35: Using MC, (KFB, K to 1 st before M, KFB, SM) four times. 152 sts, 38 between Ms.
Rnds 36–45: With MC, work Rnds 20–21 five times, switching to 24″ needle when necessary. 192 sts. See 3-Needle Bind Off instructions at end of pattern.

Row 2 Squares (make five, for Throw only)
Work as for Row 1 Squares through Rnd 27. 120 sts, 30 between Ms.
Rnd 28: P all.
Rnd 29: Using MC, (KFB, K to 1 st before M, KFB, SM) four times. 8 sts inc.
Rnds 30–45: Rep Rnds 28–29 eight more times, switching to 24″ needle when necessary. 192 sts.

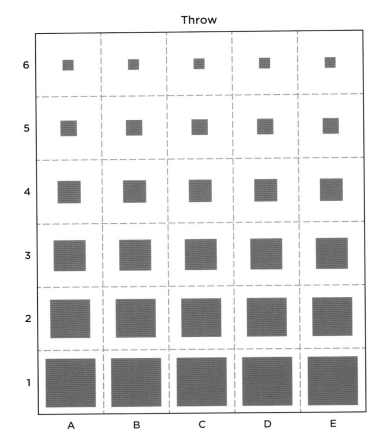

Throw

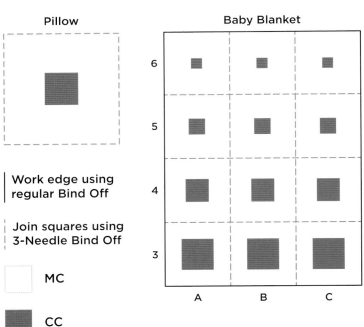

Pillow

Work edge using regular Bind Off

Join squares using 3-Needle Bind Off

☐ MC

■ CC

Baby Blanket

Row 3 Squares (make five for Throw; make three for Baby Blanket)
Work as for Row 1 Squares through Rnd 21. 96 sts, 24 between Ms.
Rnd 22: P all.
Rnd 23: Using MC, (KFB, K to 1 st before M, KFB, SM) four times. 8 sts inc.

Rnds 24–45: Rep Rnds 22–23 eleven more times, switching to 24" needle when necessary. 192 sts.

Row 4 Squares (make five for Throw; make three for Baby Blanket)

Work as for Row 1 Squares through Rnd 16. 72 sts, 18 per DPN.
Rnd 17: Using MC, (KFB, K to last st on DPN, KFB) four times. 80 sts, 20 per DPN.
Rnd 18: P all.
Rnd 19: Using 16" circular needle, (KFB, K to last st on DPN, KFB, PM) four times. Last M placed should be unique to denote BOR. 88 sts, 22 between Ms.
Rnd 20: P all.
Rnd 21: (KFB, K to 1 st before M, KFB, SM) four times. 8 sts inc.
Rnds 22–45: Rep Rnds 20–21 twelve more times, switching to 24" needle when necessary. 192 sts.

Row 5 Squares (make five for Throw; make three for Baby Blanket)

Work as for Row 1 Squares through Rnd 9. 48 sts, 12 per DPN.
Rnd 10: P all.
Rnd 11: Using MC, (KFB, K to last st on DPN, KFB) four times. 8 sts inc.
Rnds 12–16: Rep Rnds 10–11 two more times, then Rnd 10 once more. 72 sts, 18 per DPN.
Rnds 17–45: Work as for Row 4 Squares.

Row 6 Squares (make five for Throw; make three for Baby Blanket)

Work as for Row 1 Squares through Rnd 3. 24 sts, 6 per DPN.
Rnd 4: P all.
Rnd 5: Using MC, (KFB, K to last st on DPN, KFB) four times. 8 sts inc.
Rnds 6–16: Rep Rnds 4–5 five more times, then Rnd 4 once more. 72 sts, 18 per DPN.
Rnds 17–45: Work as for Row 4 Squares.

Pillow Squares (make two for Pillow)

Work as for Row 1 Squares through Rnd 21. 96 sts, 24 between Ms.
Rnd 22: P all.
Rnd 23: Using MC, (KFB, K to 1 st before M, KFB, SM) four times. 8 sts inc.
Rnds 24–81: Rep Rnds 22–23 29 more times, switching to 24" and 32" needles when necessary. 336 sts, 84 between Ms. Move sts from first square to scrap yarn.

3-Needle Bind Off for Throw

Square 1A: BO sts to next M, RM. BO sts to second M, 1 st remaining on RH needle. Break yarn with 18" tail and pull through st on RH needle, RM. Move next 48 sts to SY, RM. Move next 48 sts to SY, RM.
Squares 1B, 1C & 1D: Arrange square so it aligns with adjoining square as in diagram. Move 48 sts from adjoining square to spare circular needle. Hold next 48 sts with 48 sts from adjoining square so RS face each other and WS face out; 3NBO to next M, RM. Regular BO all sts to second M, 1 st remaining on RH needle. Break yarn with 18" tail and pull through st on RH needle, RM. Move next 48 sts to SY, RM.

Move next 48 sts to SY, RM.

Square 1E: Arrange square so it aligns with adjoining square as in diagram. Move 48 sts from adjoining square to spare circular needle. Hold next 48 sts with 48 sts from adjoining square so RS face each other and WS face out; 3NBO to next M, RM. Regular BO all sts to second M, RM. Regular BO all sts to third M, 1 st remaining on RH needle. Break yarn with 18" tail and pull through st on RH needle, RM. Move next 48 sts to SY, RM.

Square 2A: BO sts to next M, RM. Arrange square so it aligns with adjoining square as in diagram. Move 48 sts from adjoining square to spare circular needle. Hold next 48 sts with 48 sts from adjoining square so RS face each other and WS face out; 3NBO to next M, 1 st remaining on RH needle. Break yarn with 18" tail and pull through st on RH needle, RM. Move next 48 sts to SY, RM. Move next 48 sts to SY, RM.
Squares 2B, 2C & 2D: Arrange square so it aligns with adjoining squares as in diagram. Move 48 sts from two adjoining squares to spare circular needle. Hold next 48 sts with 48 sts from first adjoining square so RS face each other and WS face out; 3NBO to next M, RM. 3NBO to second M, 1 st remaining on RH needle. Break yarn with 18" tail and pull through st on RH needle, RM. Move next 48 sts to SY, RM. Move next 48 sts to SY, RM.
Square 2E: Arrange square so it aligns with adjoining squares as in diagram. Move 48 sts from two adjoining squares to spare circular needle. Hold next 48 sts with 48 sts from first adjoining square so RS face each other and WS face out; 3NBO to next M, RM. 3NBO to second M, RM. Regular BO all sts to third M, 1 st remaining on RH needle. Break yarn with 18" tail and pull through st on RH needle, RM. Move next 48 sts to SY, RM.

Square 3A: Work as for Square 2A.
Squares 3B, 3C & 3D: Work as for Square 2B.
Square 3E: Work as for Square 2E.

Square 4A: Work as for Square 2A.
Squares 4B, 4C & 4D: Work as for Square 2B.
Square 4E: Work as for Square 2E.

Square 5A: Work as for Square 2A.
Squares 5B, 5C & 5D: Work as for Square 2B.
Square 5E: Work as for Square 2E.

Square 6A: BO all sts to first M, RM. BO all sts to second M, RM. Arrange square so it aligns with adjoining squares as in diagram. Move 48 sts from adjoining square to spare circular needle. Hold next 48 sts with 48 sts from adjoining square so RS face each other and WS face out; 3NBO to next M, 1 st remaining on RH needle. Break yarn with 18" tail and pull through st on RH needle, RM. Move next 48 sts to SY, RM.
Squares 6B, 6C & 6D: BO all sts to first M, RM. Arrange square so it aligns with adjoining squares as in diagram. Move 48 sts from two adjoining squares to spare circular needle. Hold next 48 sts with 48 sts from first adjoining square so RS face each other and WS face out; 3NBO to next M, RM. 3NBO to next M, 1 st remaining on RH needle. Break yarn with 18" tail and pull through st on RH needle, RM. Move next 48 sts to SY, RM.

Square 6E: BO all sts to first M, RM. BO all sts to second M, RM. Arrange square so it aligns with adjoining squares as in diagram. Move 48 sts from two adjoining squares to spare circular needle. Hold next 48 sts with 48 sts from first adjoining square so RS face each other and WS face out; 3NBO to next M, RM. 3NBO to next M, 1 st remaining on RH needle. Break yarn with 18″ tail and pull through st on RH needle, RM.

3-Needle Bind Off for Baby Blanket
Square 3A: Use BO instructions for Throw Square 1A.
Square 3B: Use BO instructions for Throw Square 1B.
Square 3C: Use BO instructions for Throw Square 1E.

Square 4A: Use BO instructions for Throw Square 2A.
Square 4B: Use BO instructions for Throw Square 2B.
Square 4C: Use BO instructions for Throw Square 2E.

Square 5A: Use BO instructions for Throw Square 2A.
Square 5B: Use BO instructions for Throw Square 2B.
Square 5C: Use BO instructions for Throw Square 2E.

Square 6A: Use BO instructions for Throw Square 6A.
Square 6B: Use BO instructions for Throw Square 6B.
Square 6C: Use BO instructions for Throw Square 6E.

Finishing for Throw & Baby Blanket
Weave in ends, using long tails to neaten gaps where corners meet. Wash, and block to diagram.

3-Needle Bind Off for Pillow
Move sts from first square to spare needle. Hold two squares so RS face outward and WS face each other. 3NBO around 252 sts, RMs when reached.

Finishing for Pillow
Weave in ends, stuff with pillow insert, and 3NBO remaining 84 sts.

COLOR IT YOURSELF!

TRADITIONS

by Knit Picks Design Team

FINISHED MEASUREMENTS
39″ × 52″

YARN
Wool of the Andes™ Tweed (worsted weight, 80% Peruvian Highland Wool, 20% Donegal Tweed; 110 yards/50g): C1 Sea Glass Heather 28298, C2 Garnet Heather 25965, C3 Vineyard Heather 28302, C4 Cottage Heather 28301, C5 Picket Fence Heather 28309, C6 North Pole Heather 25964, 2 skeins each; C7 Wellies Heather 25968, C8 Flagstone Heather 25457, C9 Down Heather 25458, 3 skeins each

NEEDLES
US 7 (4.5mm) straight or circular needles, or size to obtain gauge

NOTIONS
Yarn Needle
Stitch Markers

GAUGE
16 sts and 32 rows = 4″ in Garter Stitch, blocked

For pattern support, contact customerservice@knitpicks.com

Traditions

Notes:

This quilt-inspired afghan is made with twelve squares, each patchwork block formed by geometric shapes that are picked up and knit off of each other.

To save yardage, keep yarn tails short. If not planning to line the back of the blanket with fabric, consider weaving in ends while knitting. Stitch and row gauge are particularly important for this pattern. It is suggested that the gauge swatch be worked in C9.

DIRECTIONS

Block A (make six)
Section 1
With C1, CO 14 sts.
Beginning with a RS row, knit 27 rows.
BO on Row 28 (WS).

Section 2
With C6, and RS facing, PU and K 14 sts along CO edge of Section 1 square. Knit 13 rows, ending on a WS row. (7 Garter ridges.) BO across next row (RS). Rep for each of the other three sides of Section 1 square, picking up into Garter Stitch bumps along sides, and into BO sts along BO edge.

Section 3
With C4, and RS facing, PU and K 7 sts along first half of BO edge of a Section 2 rectangle, beginning at RH corner.
Row 1 (WS): K2tog, K to end. 1 st dec.
Row 2 (RS): K across.
Rep Rows 1–2 four more times. 2 sts.
Next Row (WS): K2tog, break yarn, and fasten off.

With C4, and RS facing, PU and K 7 remaining sts along BO edge of Section 2 rectangle, ending in LH corner.
Row 1 (WS): K to last 2 sts, SSK. 1 st dec.
Row 2 (RS): K across.
Rep Rows 1–2 four more times. 2 sts.
Next Row (WS): SSK, break yarn, and fasten off.
Rep this whole section three more times, once for each Section 2 rectangle.

Color key:
C1
C2
C3
C4
C5
C6
C7
C8
C9

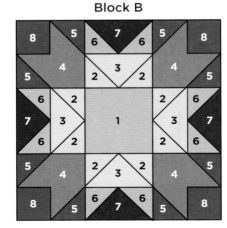

Block A

Block B

Section 4
With C3, and RS facing, PU and K 10 sts along dec edge of a Section 3 triangle, PM for center, PU and K 10 sts along dec edge of adjacent Section 3 triangle. 20 sts.

Row 1 (WS): K2tog, K to 2 sts before M, K2tog, SM, SSK, K to last 2 sts, SSK. 4 sts dec.
Row 2 (RS): K across.
Rep Rows 1–2 until 8 sts remain.
Next Row (WS): K2tog twice then SSK twice, binding off all sts as they are formed.
Rep this section three more times, once for each pair of Section 3 triangles.

Section 5

With C5, and RS facing, PU and K 14 sts along selvage edge of a Section 3 triangle and the adjacent Section 2 rectangle (ending at corner of Section 1 square), PM for center, PU and K 14 sts along selvage edge of adjacent Section 2 rectangle and Section 3 triangle, ending at peak of triangle. 28 sts.
Work Rows 1–2 as for Section 4 triangle, to BO.
Rep this section three more times, once for each corner of the Section 1 square.

Section 6

With C3, and RS facing, PU and K 10 sts along first half of edge of a Section 5 triangle, extending from RH corner to center st.
Row 1 (WS): K2tog, K to last 2 sts, SSK. 2 sts dec.
Row 2 (RS): K across.
Rep Rows 1–2 two more times. 4 sts.
Next Row (WS): K2tog, SSK. 2 sts.
Next Row (RS): K2tog, break yarn, and fasten off.

With C3, and RS facing, PU and K 10 remaining sts along edge of the Section 5 triangle, extending from center st to LH corner.
Work another triangle, same as the last one.
Rep this whole section three more times, once for each Section 5 triangle.

Section 7

With C2, and RS facing, PU and K 7 sts along inner edge of a Section 6 triangle, PM for center, PU and K 7 sts along inner edge of adjacent Section 6 triangle. 14 sts.
Row 1 (WS): K to 2 sts before M, K2tog, SM, SSK, K to end. 2 sts dec.
Row 2 (RS): K across.
Rep Rows 1–2 four more times. 4 sts.
Next Row (WS): K2tog, SSK. 2 sts.
Next Row (RS): K2tog, break yarn, and fasten off.
Rep this section three more times, once for each pair of Section 6 triangles.

Block B (make six)

Section 1
With C4, CO 14 sts.
Beginning with a RS row, knit 27 rows.
BO on Row 28 (WS).

Section 2
With C6, and RS facing, PU and K 7 sts along first half of BO edge of Section 1, beginning at RH corner.
Row 1 (WS): K2tog, K to end. 1 st dec.
Row 2 (RS): K across.

Rep Rows 1–2 four more times. 2 sts.
Next Row (WS): K2tog, break yarn, and fasten off.

With C6, and RS facing, PU and K 7 remaining sts along BO edge of Section 1, ending at LH corner.
Row 1 (WS): K to last 2 sts, SSK. 1 st dec.
Row 2 (RS): K across.
Rep Rows 1–2 four more times. 2 sts.
Next Row (WS): SSK, break yarn, and fasten off.
Rep this whole section three more times, once for each side of Section 1 square, picking up into Garter Stitch bumps along sides, and into CO loops along CO edge.

Section 3
With C5, and RS facing, PU and K 10 sts along dec edge of a Section 2 triangle, PM for center, PU and K 10 sts along dec edge of adjacent Section 2 triangle. 20 sts.
Row 1 (WS): K2tog, K to 2 sts before M, K2tog, SM, SSK, K to last 2 sts, SSK. 4 sts dec.
Row 2 (RS): K across.
Rep Rows 1–2 two more times. 8 sts.
Next Row (WS): K2tog twice then SSK twice, binding off all sts as they are formed.
Rep this section three more times, once for each pair of Section 2 triangles.

Section 4
With C1, and RS facing, PU and K 7 sts along outside edge of a Section 2 triangle (working towards corner of Section 1 square), PM for center, PU and K 7 sts along outside edge of adjacent Section 2 triangle. 14 sts.
Row 1 (WS): KFB, K to 2 sts before M, K2tog, SM, SSK, K to last st, KFB.
Row 2 (RS): K across.
Rep Rows 1–2 seven more times.
BO all sts (on WS).
Rep this section three more times, once for each pair of Section 2 triangles.

Section 5
With C2, and RS facing, PU and K 10 sts along selvage edge of Section 4 shape, beginning at corner of Section 2 triangle.
Row 1 (WS): K2tog, K to last 2 sts, SSK. 2 sts dec.
Row 2 (RS): K across.
Rep Rows 1–2 two more times. 4 sts.
Next Row (WS): K2tog, SSK. 2 sts.
Next Row (RS): K2tog, break yarn, and fasten off.
Rep this section seven more times, once for each Section 4 selvage edge; on mirrored reps, PU will end at Section 2 triangle corner instead of beginning there.

Section 6
With C4, and RS facing, PU and K 7 sts along LH edge of Section 3 triangle (beginning at center of Section 3 edge), PM for center, PU and K 7 sts along edge of adjacent Section 5 triangle. 14 sts.
Row 1 (WS): K2tog, K to 2 sts before M, K2tog, SM, SSK, K to last 2 sts, SSK. 4 sts dec.
Row 2 (RS): K across.

Rep Rows 1–2 once more. 6 sts.

Next Row (WS): K2tog twice then SSK, binding off all sts as they are formed.

Rep this section seven more times, once for each intersection of Sections 3 and 5; on mirrored reps, PU first 7 sts along Section 5 edge, next 7 sts along adjacent Section 3 RH edge.

Section 7

With C3, and RS facing, PU and K 10 sts along diagonal edge of a Section 6 triangle, PM for center, PU and K 10 sts along diagonal edge of adjacent Section 6 triangle. 20 sts.

Row 1 (WS): K2tog, K to 2 sts before M, K2tog, SM, SSK, K to last 2 sts, SSK. 4 sts dec.

Row 2 (RS): K across.

Rep Rows 1–2 two more times. 8 sts.

Next Row (WS): K2tog twice then SSK twice, binding off all sts as they are formed.

Rep this section three more times, once for each pair of Section 6 triangles.

Section 8

With C2, and RS facing, PU and K 7 sts along first half of BO edge of a Section 4 shape, PM for center, PU and K 7 remaining BO sts. 14 sts.

Row 1 (WS): K to 2 sts before M, K2tog, SM, SSK, K to end. 2 sts dec.

Row 2 (RS): K across.

Rep Rows 1–2 four more times. 4 sts.

Next Row (WS): K2tog, SSK. 2 sts.

Next Row (RS): K2tog, break yarn, and fasten off.

Rep this section three more times, once for each Section 4 shape edge.

Borders

Note: Border instructions are identical for Block A and Block B. Rep the following instructions twelve times, once for each block. See Border Application diagram for clarification.

Step 1. Beginning on any side of a block, *with C9, and RS facing, PU and K 42 sts.
Knit two rows. BO K-wise.

Step 2. Moving to side of block directly across from side just worked, with C9, rep Step 1 from *.

Step 3. Moving to one of the sides not yet worked, *with C9, and RS facing, PU and K 46 sts.
Knit two rows. BO K-wise.

Step 4. Moving to side of block directly across from side just worked, with C9, rep Step 3 from *.

Step 5. Along side of block where first border strip was worked, *with C8, and RS facing, PU and K 46 sts.
Knit two rows. BO in K-wise.

Step 6. Moving to the side of the block directly across from the side just worked, with C8, rep Step 5 from *.

Step 7. Moving to one of the sides not yet worked, *with C8, and RS facing, PU and K 50 sts.
Knit two rows. BO K-wise.

Border Application

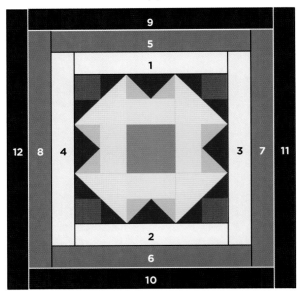

border is not to scale with block

Step 8. Moving to side of block directly across from side just worked, with C8, rep Step 7 from *.

Step 9. Along side of block where first border strip was worked, *with C7, and RS facing, PU and K 50 sts.
Knit one row. BO K-wise.

Step 10. Moving to side of block directly across from side just worked, with C7, rep Step 9 from *.

Step 11. Moving to one of the sides not yet worked, *with C7, and RS facing, PU and K 52 sts.
Knit one row. BO K-wise.

Step 12. Moving to side of block directly across from side just worked, with C7, rep Step 11 from *.

Finishing

Seam blocks tog with C7, following full blanket diagram. Weave in remaining ends. Block to measurements.

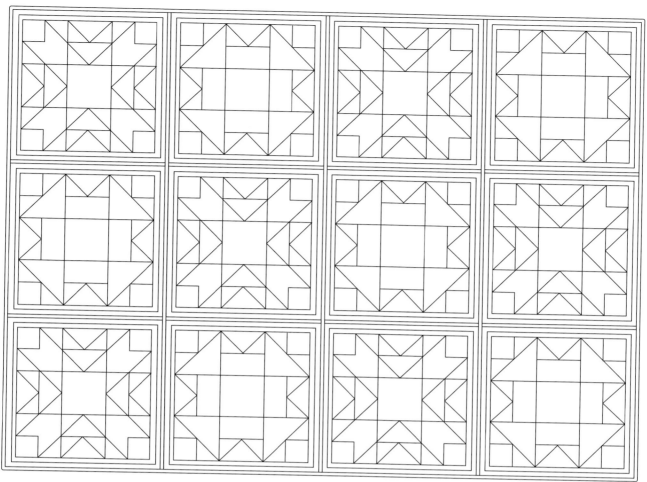

COLOR IT YOURSELF!

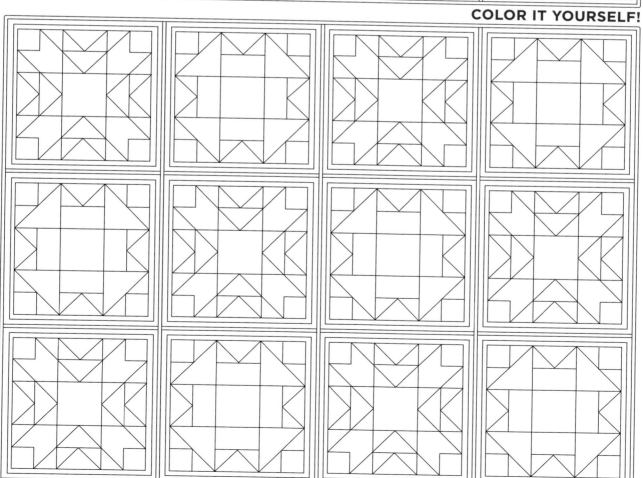

Glossary
Common Stitches & Techniques

Slipped Stitches (Sl)
Always slip stitches purl-wise with yarn held to the wrong side of work, unless noted otherwise in the pattern.

Make 1 Left-Leaning Stitch (M1L)
Inserting LH needle from front to back, PU the horizontal strand between the st just worked and the next st, and K TBL.

Make 1 Right-Leaning Stitch (M1R)
Inserting LH needle from back to front, PU the horizontal strand between the st just worked and the next st, and K TFL.

Slip, Slip, Knit (SSK)
(Sl1 K-wise) twice; insert LH needle into front of these 2 sts and knit them together.

Centered Double Decrease (CDD)
Slip first and second sts together as if to work K2tog; K1; pass 2 slipped sts over the knit st.

Stockinette Stitch (St st, flat over any number of sts)
Row 1 (RS): Knit all sts.
Row 2 (WS): Purl all sts.
Rep Rows 1-2 for pattern.
St st in the round: Knit every rnd.

Garter Stitch (in the round over any number of sts)
Rnd 1: Purl all sts.
Rnd 2: Knit all sts.
Rep Rnds 1-2 for pattern.
Garter Stitch flat: Knit every row.
(One Garter ridge is comprised of two rows/rnds.)

1x1 Rib (flat or in the round, over an even number of sts)
Row/Rnd 1: (K1, P1) to end of row/rnd.
Rep Row/Rnd 1 for pattern.

2x2 Rib (flat over a multiple of 4 sts plus 2)
Row 1 (RS): K2, (P2, K2) to end of row.
Row 2 (WS): P2, (K2, P2) to end of row.
Rep Rows 1-2 for pattern.

2x2 Rib (in the round over a multiple of 4 sts)
Rnd 1: (K2, P2) to end of rnd.
Rep Rnd 1 for pattern.

Magic Loop Technique
A technique using one long circular needle to knit in the round around a small circumference. A tutorial can be found at tutorials.knitpicks.com/wptutorials/magic-loop.

Knitting in the Round with Two Circular Needles
A technique using two long circulars to knit around a small circumference. A tutorial can be found at tutorials.knitpicks.com/knitting-in-the-round-with-2-circular-needles.

Backward Loop Cast On
A simple, all-purpose cast on that can be worked mid-row. Also called Loop, Single, or E-Wrap Cast On. A tutorial can be found at tutorials.knitpicks.com/loop-cast-on.

Long Tail Cast On
Fast and neat once you get the hang of it. Also referred to as the Slingshot Cast On. A tutorial can be found at tutorials.knitpicks.com/long-tail-cast-on.

Cabled Cast On
A strong and nice looking basic cast on that can be worked mid-project. A tutorial can be found at tutorials.knitpicks.com/cabled-cast-on.

3-Needle Bind Off
Used to easily seam two rows of live stitches together. A tutorial can be found at tutorials.knitpicks.com/3-needle-bind-off.

Abbreviations

approx	approximately	KFB	knit into front and back of stitch	PSSO	pass slipped stitch over
BO	bind off	K-wise	knit-wise	PU	pick up
BOR	beginning of round	LH	left hand	P-wise	purl-wise
CN	cable needle	M	marker	rep	repeat
C (1, 2...)	color (1, 2...)	M1	make 1 stitch	Rev St st	reverse stockinette stitch
CC	contrast color	M1L	make 1 left-leaning stitch (*see above*)	RH	right hand
CDD	centered double decrease (*see above*)	M1R	make 1 right-leaning stitch (*see above*)	rnd(s)	round(s)
				RS	right side
CO	cast on			Sk	skip
cont	continue	MC	main color	SK2P	slip 1, knit 2 together, pass slipped stitch over
dec(s)	decrease(es)	P	purl		
DPN(s)	double pointed needle(s)	P2tog	purl 2 stitches together	SKP	slip, knit, pass slipped stitch over
inc(s)	increase(es)	P3tog	purl 3 stitches together	Sl	slip (*see above*)
K	knit			SM	slip marker
K2tog	knit 2 stitches together	PM	place marker	SSK	slip, slip, knit these 2 stitches together (*see above*)
K3tog	knit 3 stitches together	PFB	purl into front and back of stitch		

SSP	slip, slip, purl these 2 stitches together through back loop		
SSSK	slip, slip, slip, knit these 3 stitches together (like SSK)		
St st	stockinette stitch (*see above*)		
st(s)	stitch(es)		
TBL	through back loop		
TFL	through front loop		
tog	together		
W&T	wrap & turn (for short rows; *see next pg*)		
WE	work even		
WS	wrong side		
WYIB	with yarn in back		
WYIF	with yarn in front		
YO	yarn over		

Cables (Including without a Cable Needle)

Tutorials for 1 over 1 cables can be found at blog.knitpicks.com/tutorial-1-over-1-cables-without-a-cable-needle. Tutorials for standard cables can be found at blog.knitpicks.com/tutorial-introduction-to-cables.

Felted Join (to splice yarn)

One method for joining a new length of yarn to the end of one that is already being used. A tutorial can be found at tutorials.knitpicks.com/felted-join.

Mattress Stitch

A neat, invisible seaming method that uses the bars between the first and second stitches on the edges. A tutorial can be found at tutorials.knitpicks.com/mattress-stitch.

Provisional Cast On (crochet method)

Used to cast on stitches that are also a row of live stitches, so they can be put onto a needle and used later.

Directions: Using a crochet hook, make a slip knot, then hold knitting needle in left hand, hook in right. With yarn in back of needle, work a chain st by pulling yarn over needle and through chain st. Move yarn back to behind needle, and rep for the number of sts required. Chain a few more sts off the needle, then break yarn and pull end through last chain. (CO sts may be incorrectly mounted; if so, work into backs of these sts.) To unravel later (when sts need to be picked up), pull chain end out; chain should unravel, leaving live sts. A video tutorial can be found at tutorials.knitpicks.com/crocheted-provisional-cast-on.

Provisional Cast On (crochet chain method)

Same result as the crochet method above, but worked differently, so you may prefer one or the other.

Directions: With a crochet hook, use scrap yarn to make a slip knot and chain the number of sts to be cast on, plus a few extra sts. Insert tip of knitting needle into first bump of crochet chain. Wrap project yarn around needle as if to knit, and pull yarn through crochet chain, forming first st. Rep this process until you have cast on the correct number of sts. To unravel later (when sts need to be picked up), pull chain out, leaving live sts. A photo tutorial can be found at tutorials.knitpicks.com/crocheted-provisional-cast-on.

Judy's Magic Cast On

This method creates stitches coming out in opposite directions from a seamless center line, perfect for starting toe-up socks.

Directions: Make a slip knot and place loop around one of the two needles; anchor loop counts as first st. Hold needles tog, with needle that yarn is attached to on top. In other hand, hold yarn so tail goes over index finger and yarn attached to ball goes over thumb. Bring tip of bottom needle over strand of yarn on finger (top strand), around and under yarn and back up, making a loop around needle. Pull loop snug. Bring top needle (with slip knot) over yarn tail on thumb (bottom strand), around and under yarn and back up, making a loop around needle. Pull loop snug. Cont casting on sts until desired number is reached; top yarn strand always wraps around bottom needle, and bottom yarn strand always wraps around top needle. A tutorial can be found at tutorials.knitpicks.com/judys-magic-cast-on.

Stretchy Bind Off

Directions: K2, *insert LH needle into front of 2 sts on RH needle and knit them tog—1 st remains on RH needle. K1; rep from * until all sts have been bound off. A tutorial can be found at tutorials.knitpicks.com/go-your-own-way-socks-toe-up-part-7-binding-off.

Jeny's Surprisingly Stretchy Bind Off (for 1x1 Rib)

Directions: Reverse YO, K1, pass YO over; *YO, P1, pass YO and previous st over P1; reverse YO, K1, pass YO and previous st over K1; rep from * until 1 st is left, then break working yarn and pull it through final st to complete BO.

Kitchener Stitch (also called Grafting)

Seamlessly join two sets of live stitches together.

Directions: With an equal number of sts on two needles, break yarn leaving a tail approx four times as long as the row of sts, and thread through a blunt yarn needle. Hold needles parallel with WSs facing in and both needles pointing to the right. Perform Step 2 on the first front st, then Step 4 on the first back st, then continue from Step 1, always pulling yarn tightly so the grafted row tension matches the knitted fabric:

Step 1: Pull yarn needle K-wise through front st and drop st from knitting needle.

Step 2: Pull yarn needle P-wise through next front st, leaving st on knitting needle.

Step 3: Pull yarn needle P-wise through first back st and drop st from knitting needle.

Step 4: Pull yarn needle K-wise through next back st, leaving st on knitting needle.

Rep Steps 1-4 until all sts have been grafted together, finishing by working Step 1 through the last remaining front st, then Step 3 through the last remaining back st. Photo tutorials can be found at knitpicks.com/learning-center/learn-to-knit/kitchener.

Short Rows

There are several options for how to handle short rows, so you may see different suggestions/intructions in a pattern.

Wrap and Turn (W&T) (one option for Short Rows)

Work until the st to be wrapped. If knitting: Bring yarn to front, Sl next st P-wise, return yarn to back; turn work, and Sl wrapped st onto RH needle. Cont across row. If purling: Bring yarn to back of work, Sl next st P-wise, return yarn to front; turn work and Sl wrapped st onto RH needle. Cont across row.

Picking up Wraps: Work to wrapped st. If knitting: Insert RH needle under wrap, then through wrapped st K-wise; K st and wrap tog. If purling: Sl wrapped st P-wise onto RH needle, use LH needle to lift wrap and place it onto RH needle; Sl wrap and st back onto LH needle, and P tog.

A tutorial for W&T can be found at tutorials.knitpicks.com/short-rows-wrap-and-turn-or-wt.

German Short Rows (another option for Short Rows)

Work to turning point; turn. WYIF, Sl first st P-wise. Bring yarn over back of right needle, pulling firmly to create a "double stitch" on RH needle. If next st is a K st, leave yarn at back; if next st is a P st, bring yarn to front between needles. When it's time to work into double st, knit both strands tog.

THIS COLLECTION FEATURES

Brava™
Worsted Weight
100% Premium Acrylic

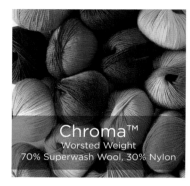

Chroma™
Worsted Weight
70% Superwash Wool, 30% Nylon

Mighty Stitch™
Worsted & Bulky Weights
80% Acrylic 20% Superwash Wool

Swish™
Worsted & DK Weights
100% Fine Superwash Merino Wool

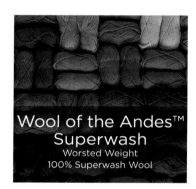

Wool of the Andes™ Superwash
Worsted Weight
100% Superwash Wool

Wool of the Andes™ Tweed
Worsted Weight
80% Peruvian Highland Wool,
20% Donegal Tweed

View these beautiful
yarns and more at
www.KnitPicks.com

Knit Picks yarn is both luxe and affordable—a seeming contradiction
trounced! But it's not just about the pretty colors; we also care
deeply about fiber quality and fair labor practices, leaving you with
a gorgeously reliable product you'll turn to time and time again.